GREATER
THAN YOU
THINK

GREATER THAN YOU THINK

A Theologian Answers the Atheists About God

THOMAS D. WILLIAMS, LC, ThD

New York   Boston   Nashville

Unless otherwise noted, Scripture quotations are from the New Revised Standard Version Bible, copyright © 1989, by the Division of Christian Education of the National Council of the Churches of Christ in the United States of America. All rights reserved.

Scripture quotations noted NIV are from the Holy Bible, New International Version®. Copyright © 1973, 1978, 1984 by International Bible Society. Used by permission of Zondervan Publishing House. All rights reserved. The "NIV" and "New International Version" trademarks are registered in the United States Patent and Trademark Office by International Bible Society. Use of either trademark requires the permission of International Bible Society.

Scriptures noted RSV are from the REVISED STANDARD VERSION of the Bible. Copyright © 1952, 1971 by the Division of Christian Education of the National Council of Churches of Christ in the United States of America. Used by permission.

Scriptures noted NAB are from the New American Bible. Copyright © 1987 by Thomas Nelson, Inc. Revised New Testament copyright © 1986 by the Confraternity of Christian Doctrine, Washington, D.C. All rights reserved.

FaithWords
Hachette Book Group USA
237 Park Avenue
New York, NY 10017

Visit our Web site at www.faithwords.com.

Printed in the United States of America

First Edition: June 2008

10 9 8 7 6 5 4 3 2 1

FaithWords is a division of Hachette Book Group USA, Inc.
The FaithWords name and logo are trademarks of Hachette Book Group USA, Inc.

Library of Congress Cataloging-in-Publication Data

Williams, Thomas D., LC, ThD
Greater than you think : a theologian answers the atheists about God /
Thomas D. Williams.—1st ed.
p. cm.
ISBN-13: 978-0-446-51493-4
ISBN-10: 0-446-51493-4
1. Apologetics. I. Title.
BT1103.W545 2008
239—dc22
2007049594

Design by Meryl Sussman Levavi

Seek and you will find.

(Luke 11:9 NAB)

Contents

Introduction... xi

I: RELIGION IN THE CROSSHAIRS

1. Religion or religions?
   Are all religions the same? 5

2. Isn't religion just wishful thinking? 11

3. Does God answer our prayers?......................... 15

4. Can a person be morally good
   without religion?... 18

5. Isn't faith in God a cop-out for those
   who cannot handle mortality? 22

6. Are religious people less intelligent
   than nonbelievers?... 25

Contents

II: RELIGION AND SOCIETY

7. Does religion do more harm than good? 33

8. Doesn't religion cause war and violence? 38

9. Are religious people irresponsible citizens?.... 44

10. Are believers trying to hasten the end
    of the world?.. 48

11. Is religious education a form
    of child abuse?.. 51

12. Should believers be allowed to proselytize? 57

III: FAITH—SCIENCE—REASON

13. Hasn't science disproved God's existence?...... 67

14. Doesn't the Bible misrepresent the origins
    of man and the cosmos? 73

15. Is Christianity against science? 79

16. Aren't all scientists and thinking people
    atheists, or at least agnostics?........................... 85

17. Is religious faith irrational?.............................. 90

IV: CHRISTIANITY UNDER FIRE

18. Is the God of the Bible a jealous sadist?......... 101

19. Are the Gospels reliable historical
    documents? 107

CONTENTS

20. Did the historical Jesus really exist?............... 112

21. Did Jesus found the church, or was He
    co-opted by His followers?................................. 117

22. Do Christians hate sex? Does faith
    encourage sexual repression? 121

V: ATHEISM UNDER THE MICROSCOPE

23. Are atheists more tolerant than believers?..... 131

24. Are atheists better citizens than religious
    folk? 136

25. Are atheists more ethical than religious
    believers? 140

26. Are atheists happier than believers?.............. 148

27. Are atheists more generous and philanthropic
    than their religious counterparts?................. 152

    Epilogue: An Appeal to Christians............... 157

    Notes... 161

    About the Author... 173

Introduction

UNLESS YOU'VE SPENT THE LAST FEW YEARS IN A mountain hermitage, you have almost certainly run into the latest rash of anti-God books. And a rash it is, since the very mention of a Supreme Being makes atheists break out in hives. But they are scratching all the way to the bank, as several of these recent diatribes have become bestsellers, showing once again that religion-bashing never truly goes out of style.

The list includes Richard Dawkins's *The God Delusion* (2006), Sam Harris's *The End of Faith: Religion, Terror, and the Future of Reason* (2005) and his *Letter to a Christian Nation* (2006), Daniel C. Dennett's *Breaking the Spell: Religion as a Natural Phenomenon*

(2006), and journalist Christopher Hitchens's 2007 work *God Is Not Great: How Religion Poisons Everything*. These bestsellers are accompanied by reams of lesser works, attesting to the power of atheism as the newest cottage industry.

Though their arguments are not new, the neo-atheists require a reasoned response. If nothing else, their very popularity means that many people are exposed to the objections they raise, without necessarily hearing the other side of the story. In this book I have distilled the chief arguments found in these recent atheistic texts into a series of simple questions, to which I furnish a brief response. I have tried to do so with fairness and objectivity, appealing not only to faith but especially to reason—which should be the common ground of believers and nonbelievers.

I have further subdivided the questions into five sections, to help readers address these objections in a more orderly fashion. The first section addresses *religion itself* as a human and cultural phenomenon. What problems does faith in God come up against? Second, I look at *religion and society*. Does religion make for disloyal citizens and cause wars, as the atheists contend, or does it affect society for the better? Third, I examine the relationship between *faith and science and reason*, to get a better sense of how faith and reason get along. Fourth, I explore the allegations against *Christianity in particular,* and answer the objections made to the presence of the church in the last two thousand years. Finally, I turn the tables on the atheists for a moment and investigate just *how atheism stands up* to the same questions asked of religion. Does atheism create a more faithful, generous citizenry, or does it encourage egotism and self-indulgence?

I have known a good number of atheists and agnostics in my life, and my own limited experience indicates that atheism—especially in its more passionate strain—always has its causes. All the convinced atheists I know do not merely *disbelieve* in God; they *hate* Him. He becomes for them an object not of simple indifference, but of the most visceral animosity. And this animosity seems always motivated by one of two things: a deep injustice suffered, for which they blame God and cannot forgive Him; or a deep injustice they have committed, for which they cannot forgive themselves. It happens with a truly remarkable frequency that I speak with a self-declared atheist who reveals, after some time of conversation, that "I stopped going to church after I had an abortion when I was twenty-two," or "I lost my wife when we had been married only three years," or "I stopped believing in God when my twin brother was taken from me when we were only fifteen."

I enjoy no personal friendship with any of the authors of the atheistic works being considered here, and I am not privy to sufficient details of their private lives to confidently identify the underlying causes of their hatred of God. What I can assert with moral certainty is that atheism is not natural—it is produced. What requires explanation is not how a person becomes a believer, but how a person becomes an atheist. In fact, I have never known an atheist who could not identify the event or events that brought about his or her unbelief.

I am convinced that atheism—unlike religious indifference—never represents a gentle estrangement from God or a gradual falling away from belief. It is a *rejection* of God. No one writes angry books about other phenomena in which they do *not believe*. Only God, the Supreme Deity, evokes such vehemence. Only God merits book after book of passionate denial of His existence. Only God—and especially the Christian God—invites such devotion and love on the one hand, and such deep-seated odium on the other.

Before getting to the meat of this book I must come clean regarding my own beliefs and motivations. I am first of all a Christian. That is, I believe in God, the Father Almighty, Creator of all that is, who is Love, and who loved humanity so much that He sent His only Son, Jesus Christ, into the world to be our

Savior. I believe that this Jesus became a man for us to teach us what it means to be fully human, to reveal to us God's nature as a loving communion of persons—Father, Son, and Holy Spirit—and to die for us on a cross. I believe that this Jesus rose from the dead, ascended into heaven, sent His Holy Spirit to guide us to the fullness of truth, and founded a community of believers—the church—to witness His love to the world.

There—I have set forth the core of my own faith. My Christian faith does not make me superior to anyone else. If anything, it makes me more accountable before God. I am a "cradle Christian," who from an early age recognized God's loving presence in my life. Despite my many and persistent failings, God somehow continues to love me and shower me with His grace. I will be judged according to my response to God's love in my life, and I pray that He will be merciful to me.

If anything positive can result from these atheistic writings, it is this: they offer believers an opportunity to set forth with greater clarity the reasons underlying their faith. They may also lead believers to an examination of conscience. Aren't many of the stereotypes of religion caused or abetted by the way some believers—perhaps ourselves—misrepresent religion, and by our failing to live up to our own ideals? If, for instance, all Christians were truly recognizable by their love for one another—as Christ said we should be—wouldn't nonbelievers have an easier time overcoming their prejudices concerning religious faith?

I have subtitled this book *A Theologian Answers the Atheists About God.* I answer the objections they put forth, which may or may not be the *reasons* for their atheism, but do constitute the message they send to readers. I write this book for the many "searchers" who honestly pursue their own quest for God, and who may feel put off by the supposed reasons for unbelief set forth in these tracts. I also write it for believers, especially those Christians who lack ready replies for those who come at them with such protests. I hope to supply them with the answers they seek and in this way to respond to the call of the great apostle Peter, who urged Christians: "Always be ready to make your defense to anyone who demands from you an accounting for the hope that is in you" (1 Peter 3:15).

At times I will seem dismissive of the arguments I engage. I do so not out of disrespect for those who hold them; rather, I desire their reconciliation with God as I desire everyone's reconciliation with Him. Jesus did promise, after all, that all who truly *seek* will *find.*

GREATER
THAN YOU
THINK

PART I

RELIGION IN THE CROSSHAIRS

Our first section deals with objections to religion itself as a human phenomenon. As we will immediately see, some clarification is needed as to what is meant by "religion," since the word covers a multitude of related–but often very different–beliefs systems and institutions. When Christopher Hitchens writes that "religion kills," or "religion poisons everything," or suggests that religion is "child abuse," what does he mean by "religion"?

Next we will look at atheistic authors' appropriation of Freud's theory of religion as wish fulfillment, and the idea that God's existence is a psychological projection of our need for *a father figure. Is there any empirical data to justify this theory? Is God merely a creation of humanity's collective imagination to fill a need, or could He be real? Does God's conformity to human needs and desires mean that we created Him, or could it mean that He created us?*

We will next examine the criticism that God doesn't answer people's prayers and explore the nature of prayer itself. Can God's relationship with human beings be measured by statistical analysis? What does it mean to request something from God, or for God to answer? What of all the people who say that God does answer their prayers—are they delusional?

Another area to be explored is the relationship between religion and morality. Can a person be morally good without religion? Does religion encourage morality, or is religion itself, again in Christopher Hitchens's words, "not only amoral, but immoral"?[1] Does religion bolster our natural moral inclinations or corrupt them?

A final presumption to be addressed refers to the intelligence of believers. Are religious people— as our atheists assert—less intelligent than nonbelievers? Is there some link between IQ and religious belief, or can faith be found all along the spectrum of human intelligence? These are some of the topics to be dealt with. Without further ado, let the debate begin!

1.

Religion or religions?
Are all religions the same?

CHRISTOPHER HITCHENS MINCES NO WORDS IN HIS acerbic description of "religion." In *God Is Not Great* he writes that organized religion is "violent, irrational, intolerant, allied to racism and tribalism and bigotry, invested in ignorance and hostile to free inquiry, contemptuous of women and coercive toward children."[1] Presumably all religions and all religious people exhibit these odious traits. Hitchens and his coirreligionist writers continually refer to "religion" or "organized religion" as if it were a single, undifferentiated, identifiable phenomenon. Richard Dawkins says quite explicitly: "I am not attacking any particular version of God or gods. I am attacking God, all gods, anything and everything supernatural, wherever and whenever they may have been or will be invented."[2]

Daniel Dennett defines *religion* as "social systems whose participants avow belief in a supernatural agent or agents whose approval is to be sought."[3] Yet dealing with "religion" as a simple phenomenon is highly problematic, since religions differ from one another just as people do. To illustrate this important fact, let's briefly examine two well-known believers, who both qualify as religious, according to Daniel Dennett's definition of *religion*.

David Berkowitz, better known as "Son of Sam," was a notorious serial killer who terrorized New Yorkers from July 29, 1976, until August 10, 1977, the day he was apprehended by police. He was also deeply "religious." Berkowitz famously claimed that a neighbor's dog was possessed by a demon that commanded Berkowitz to kill.

In the spring of 1975, Berkowitz had joined a violent satanic cult. The cult had roughly two dozen core members in New York, referred to by Berkowitz as the "twenty-two disciples of hell." According to his testimony, initially the group participated in harmless activities such as séances and fortune-telling. Gradually, however, Berkowitz claimed that the group introduced him to hard drug use, sadistic pornography, and violent activities. They began by killing dogs, mostly German shepherds. Then Berkowitz started killing human beings. In the end, Berkowitz shot thirteen people, six of whom died.

Our second example of a "religious" person is slightly different. Father Damien of Molokai was a Roman Catholic priest from Belgium and a member of a missionary religious order. Damien was sent to serve the people of Hawaii and on March 19, 1864, landed at Honolulu Harbor. He arrived just as the kingdom faced a public health crisis, due to diseases—including leprosy—introduced to the Hawaiian Islands by foreign traders and sailors.

Fearful of its spread, Hawaiian king Kamehameha V segregated the lepers of the kingdom and moved them to a settlement colony on the north side of the island of Molokai. Father Damien was assigned to the Catholic mission in North Kohala on Hawaii's Big Island to minister to their needs. Though he realized that this assignment could be a death sentence, after prayerful thought, Damien asked the bishop, Louis Maigret, for permission to go to Molokai.

On arriving, Damien found a morally deprived, lawless death colony, where people were obliged to fight each other to survive. Damien's first course of action was to build a church, but along with his spiritual work, Damien dressed ulcers, built homes and beds, and even constructed coffins and dug graves. Under his leadership, basic laws were enforced, shacks became painted houses, working farms were organized, and schools were erected.

Even after discovering in 1884 that he had contracted leprosy, Damien continued to work vigorously to build as many homes as he could and planned for the continuation of the programs he created after he was gone. Father Damien died at the age of forty-nine from leprosy. Later Mahatma Gandhi praised Damien's life and work, and claimed that Damien had inspired his social campaigns in India that led to the freedom of his people. Gandhi said, "The political and journalistic world can boast of very few heroes who compare with Father Damien of Molokai."[4]

People sometimes do terrible things in the name of religion. Other times they do wonderful and heroic things. When Hitchens writes chapters titled "Religion Kills," or "How Religion Poisons Everything," we are led to believe that he is referring to a single phenomenon called "religion," but is he? The examples he uses say something different. At one point he is speaking of Christians, at another point of Hindus, and more often than not he is speaking of Muslims.

Christopher Hitchens takes the very title of his book *God Is Not Great* from the words Saddam Hussein had inscribed on the Iraqi flag: *Allahuh Akhbar* ("God Is Great").[5] In so doing he equates all religion to Islamic fanaticism. He uses Islam as a weapon for bashing Christianity and Judaism. Yet it is disingenuous to speak of individual crimes as flowing from "religion," as if religion were a univocal phenomenon. In point of fact, which Hitchens should realize from his work as a journalist, *religion* means a multitude of things.

What if Hitchens were to title a chapter "Americans Kill" or "How Americans Poison Everything"? Where it is true that *some* Americans kill, it is a logical fallacy to extend that statement to *all* Americans or to infer that the reason these people kill is *because* they are Americans. This intentional ambiguity of expression spoils the scholarship of Hitchens's work and makes his conclusions extremely suspicious.

Had Christopher Hitchens subtitled his book "How Fanaticism Poisons Everything," he would have had a leg to stand on. Religious extremism—like all extremism—is often a dangerous phenomenon. All of his examples, in fact, come from religious extremists, who often contravene their own moral codes in their crimes. But by lumping all religious belief together, as if "religion" were one monolithic, homogeneous whole, Hitchens muddles the issue rather than clarifying it. Fine, you can put Rasputin and Mother Teresa, Richard Ramirez and Mahatma Gandhi together in the category of "religious" people, but what did they really have in common, other than a belief in the supernatural? Nothing at all.

What readers should have very clear is that talk of crimes of "religion" camouflages a much more complex reality.

2.

Isn't religion just wishful thinking?

THE CLAIM THAT RELIGION ARISES OUT OF WISH fulfillment constitutes for Christopher Hitchens one of the four "irreducible objections" to religious faith.[1] In other words, this is one of four insurmountable barriers that keep him from believing. More than two hundred years ago Voltaire wrote: "If God did not exist, it would be necessary to invent him,"[2] and for Hitchens that seems to mean we *must have* invented Him.

At first blush this theory makes perfect sense. After all, we would all like to believe that there is a Supreme Being who made us, who loves us, and who will provide ultimate justice after death. This Divinity fills in many of the holes that bother us about our earthly existence. The quandaries over suffering, death, and injustice, and our longing for a happiness that will never end, jibe nicely with the idea of a loving, omnipotent father figure.

Yet the fact that many aspects of our understanding of the Divinity coincide with the human heart's deepest longings really furnishes no new information concerning His possible existence. If there is a God, it would make good sense for Him to create us in such a way that we long for exactly what He provides. Our desires for food and human companionship don't mean that filet mignon and friendship are projections of the human imagination.

Remember, too, that just as we have motivations to believe in God, plenty of people have strong motivations to *disbelieve*. What, for instance, of those who don't relish the idea of an ultimate justice after death? What of those who don't particularly care for the rules that God lays down regarding their conduct? What of those who simply don't want an authority figure—benign or otherwise—interfering with their absolute autonomy and independence?

In what way, then, could the wish-fulfillment theory possibly reach the status of an "irreducible objection"? At most it provides one of many possible explanations of how people come to believe in God. It says nothing about the existence of God.

Hitchens's objection comes from Sigmund Freud's hypothesis that God is a psychological projection of our need for a perfect father figure. In his work *Totem and Taboo,* Freud wrote that a person's "relationship to God depends on the relation to his father in the flesh, and...at bottom God is nothing other than an exalted father."[3] Yet some psychologists have raised serious questions about the validity of Freud's theory. In 1999, Dr. Paul Vitz of New York University published an important study on the psychology of atheism titled *Faith of the Fatherless.*[4] Vitz found that with astounding frequency, atheists had serious problems with their fathers. Absent, abusive, and weak father figures often went hand in hand with the phenomenon of virulent atheism. Vitz hypothesized that atheists' anger or disdain for their fathers was projected toward God and changed to rejection of the Divinity.

Contrary to the conventional Freudian wisdom that religiosity was an unnatural state in the human person that required explaining, Vitz's study found that the opposite was true: theism tends to correlate to a healthy psychology, whereas atheism arises disproportionately among those with problematic relationships with their fathers. Many factors contribute to atheism, but Vitz's study suggests that a problematic relationship with one's father may predispose to unbelief.

In short, perhaps atheism is the pathology that needs explaining, whereas theism is the natural condition of a sound psychology. Does it make more sense to suppose that every civilization known to history has been subject to collective delusion, or that perhaps a few unlucky souls resist what seems evident to everyone else?

3.

Does God answer our prayers?

O NE OF RICHARD DAWKINS'S STATED REASONS for not believing in God is that God doesn't answer our prayers. Dawkins is convinced that the existence of God can be verified or disproved using the scientific method: observation, hypothesis, experiment, and control. Therefore, if a personal God exists, He ought to behave in a logical, predictable way. As I slogged through the 416 pages of *The God Delusion,* more than once I found myself repeating the words of C. S. Lewis in reference to his Christ-figure Aslan: "But Richard, he's not a tame lion!" In other words, who says that God must behave in a way that Richard Dawkins thinks is reasonable and logical?

One of the errors made not only by Richard Dawkins, but by many Christians as well, is the assumption that God is like a pill: we take it and we feel better. Cause and effect. We pray, and we get the desired outcome, like putting a few quarters into the vending machine and out pops a can of Coca-Cola. We project a mechanistic structure onto God, as if He were not the *author* of physical laws, but *subject* to them like everything else. Yet if God is personal—and not a universal law or "force"—then it stands to reason that His responses to our entreaties will be personal, variable, and—in a divine way—*subjective.*

So what do we mean by God "answering our prayers"? Do we mean that when I ask for a red bicycle, tomorrow morning it will magically appear on my doorstep? No. Do we mean, on the other hand, that if I speak to God, tell Him of my needs and aspirations, and ask Him for His help, He hears me and *in His own way* always answers? Yes. Now I know that this reply is frustrating for Richard Dawkins and his ilk, since it takes the matter out of the empirically verifiable realm once again, yet that's just the way it is. In other words, you cannot do a prayer experiment (as Dawkins does) to prove or disprove the existence of God. You can only pray and listen. If you perceive a response, Richard Dawkins will chalk it up to wish fulfillment. That's okay. That's his prerogative.

Hundreds of thousands of people—I among them—are convinced that God not only *hears* but also *answers* our prayers. Often what first appears to be an "unanswered prayer" (you don't get the job you applied for) turns out to be an "answered prayer" (you find out that it would have been disastrous to work there). Moreover, Christian prayer does not consist in pleading our case in order to bring God around to seeing things our way. It consists more in bringing *ourselves* around to embrace God's will in our lives. In my own life, God has given me countless signs of His existence and His tender care for me. But He is not a "tame lion" and you cannot put Him in a box.

This means that I must accept His responses the way He chooses to give them, and not as I would do things in His stead. Dawkins and company would like to verify God's responsiveness to prayer—and therefore His existence or nonexistence—in a laboratory. But when it comes to prayer and its results, what is needed is the basic understanding that God is God. His response to us isn't dictated by scientific laws but by His knowledge of what is truly best for us. If we are willing to trust, we may begin to see.

4.

Can a person be morally good without religion?

THE SIMPLE ANSWER TO THIS QUESTION IS "OF course." Just as it is possible to dig a hole without a shovel, or to write a book without a computer, morality is possible without explicit religious faith. All it takes is a single example of a nonbeliever's acting morally to show that it is *possible* to do so. A more important question to ask, however, may be: "Does religious faith dispose people to act better?" Here, too, the answer is a resounding "Yes!"

Though religions vary, most have moral codes that encourage people to live better lives than they might otherwise. We are enjoined to love one another, to be humble, and to serve rather than be served. Atheists, on the other hand, have no added incentives to live morally good lives. When your ethical principles are derived from the survival of the fittest, the most you can hope for is a dog-eat-dog world. There is much sense in the dictum attributed to Fyodor Dostoyevsky: "If there is no God, everything is permitted."[1] Religious faith may not make *everyone* a better person, but it makes many people better. I'm sure you have known people who have turned their lives around, overcome vices, become better wives or husbands, and started taking their responsibilities seriously after a religious conversion. But how many people have you known that straightened out their lives because they discovered *atheism*?

It is well known that the founders of the United States believed, almost to a man, that the American experiment in ordered liberty depended upon religion. They were convinced that without belief in God, morality was impossible. In his Farewell Address of 1797, President George Washington declared that "reason and experience both forbid us to expect that national morality can prevail in exclusion of religious principle."[2] Even Thomas Jefferson, whom Richard Dawkins cites extensively (though selectively!), wrote in 1781: "God who gave us life gave us liberty. And can the liberties of a nation be thought secure when we have removed their only firm basis, a conviction in the minds of the people that these liberties are the Gift of God?"[3] And Jefferson's friend and colleague James Madison (acclaimed as the "Father of the Constitution") wrote in 1825, after retiring from the presidency, "The belief in a God All Powerful, wise and good is...essential to the moral order of the World and the happiness of men."[4]

Therefore, rather than ask whether it is possible for nonbelievers to be morally good, it makes better sense to ask: do many people behave better because of their religious faith? To this question any objective observer should answer in the affirmative.

In *God Is Not Great,* Christopher Hitchens admits he knows "a handful of priests and rabbis and imams who have put humanity ahead of their own sect or creed."[5] But this isn't the point, is it? Speaking as a Christian, I can say that I have been moved on countless occasions to put another's good ahead of my own preferences, not *in spite of,* but *because of* my Christian faith! If I weren't a Christian, what motivation would I possibly have to love my enemies, pray for my persecutors, or treat others better than they deserve—as I would wish to be treated in their place? I might do so if I found it to be useful to further my own aims, but my Christian faith urges me to do so even when it goes against my interests.

Christianity promotes morality in several ways. First, it offers an *ideal* in the person of Jesus Christ, who came "not to be served but to serve" (Matthew 20:28), who went about healing the sick, feeding the hungry, and teaching the ignorant, and who eventually gave His life for our salvation. Second, it furnishes a series of *moral injunctions*, summed up in love of God and love of neighbor, but also getting down to the nitty-gritty of how to do so. Moreover, Christians believe that God gives *His grace* to strengthen us in our resolve, allowing us to do things that we wouldn't be able to do otherwise. Finally, Christianity also provides an *eternal incentive* to do so, both as a grateful response to a loving Father and in the awareness that each of us will be judged on our conduct.

The fact that all of us fail in some way to live up to our lofty ideals doesn't negate the real moral benefits of the Christian religion. It is religious belief—and not secular humanism—that encourages us to get up again, ask pardon for our faults, and keep striving to do better.

5.

Isn't faith in God a cop-out for those who cannot handle mortality?

ALMOST EVERYONE LOOKS FOR A WAY TO OVERCOME the sobering reality of human mortality. Some look to science to extend life or possibly discover the key to immortality. Some search for a mythical "fountain of youth" to prolong years of health and happiness and thereby cheat death. Others hope to be remembered for their work, producing something of perennial value that will "live on" after them. Others look to their children and grandchildren as a way of continuing to be present in the world even after their deaths. Some believe that people are reincarnated—as plants, animals, or other persons, in an ongoing cycle of rebirth and death. Still others—

many others—harbor the hope of life after death, an eternity of bliss with a God who is both Creator and Rewarder.

A natural urge to overcome death seems deeply planted in the human spirit. Since the beginning of recorded history, men and women have instinctively rejected the idea that everything ends with death. Is this just another version of wishful thinking? Or may it just be, as Christians and many others believe, that this natural desire corresponds to a fundamental truth: death is not the end of human existence. So many other natural desires point toward something real that can satisfy the desire. We are hungry, and there is food. We are thirsty, and there is drink. We are curious, and there is knowledge to be had. We long for fellowship, and there are other people to give love and receive love. It almost seems to be a natural law that universal human desires indicate the existence of something to satisfy them. Isn't it possible that our longing for immortality is one of these?

Here, science can provide no answers. The only way to know what follows death is for someone who has experienced it to come back and tell us. People are fascinated with the reports of "near-death experiences" and the narrations of those who seemingly have crossed over to the other side. Others are skeptical, convinced that if they have come back, it means that they were not yet truly dead. Christians believe in the bodily resurrection of Jesus Christ, and in His teaching that after death the human soul lives on forever. If Jesus was God, He would have had the authority and knowledge to tell us what comes after death. Either He was, or He wasn't. At the time, many witnesses were convinced that He was telling the truth and gave their lives rather than renounce their belief. Many today continue to believe.

Some may think that Friedrich Nietzsche was right in saying that religion is a cop-out, that we should have the courage to embrace the absurdity and meaninglessness of human existence without looking further. Yet Nietzsche could just as well have been dead wrong. Sometimes we are almost too afraid to believe that God is as great as He seems, and we don't dare get our hopes up. Sometimes what our faith tells us seems too good to be true. But we must remember that sometimes wishes do come true. Some stories do have a happy ending. Some people—and God is the first among them—really do keep their promises.

6.

> ## Are religious people less intelligent than nonbelievers?

I T IS A COMMON MYTH OF OUR DAY, NOT SURPRIS-
ingly propagated by atheists, that believers are
undereducated folk who have abandoned the use of
reason in favor of blind faith. So Sam Harris writes
that because of the religious belief of its citizens, the
United States appears "like a lumbering, bellicose,
dim-witted giant."[1] It is not surprising, in fact, that
two of the atheistic authors mentioned in this book
are British, representing an island known in our day
for its religious indifference. I have lived in Europe
for seventeen years, and there is no question that
Americans' unapologetic religiosity makes Europe-
ans uncomfortable. Yet many eminent thinkers, such

as Alexis de Tocqueville, have interpreted religious conviction to be America's greatest strength.

The atheistic books are understandably well received in coastal America, which prides itself on being cosmopolitan, open-minded, and far from the credulous "Jesus land" of Middle America. Richard Dawkins states: "What is remarkable is the polar opposition between the religiosity of the American public at large and the atheism of the intellectual elite."[2] Dawkins also recently referred to the Bible Belt states as "the reptilian brain of southern and middle America," in contrast to the "country's cerebral cortex to the north and down the coasts."[3] He is right up to a point. It is well known that the coastal, semiskilled knowledge-class prides itself on its liberal, irreligious views, and that religious practice suffers on the coasts and on university campuses. What this means is up for debate. The intellectual elites were also far more susceptible than common folk to the lies of Leninist ideologies. It is also well known that, on average, serial killers have IQs far superior to those of the norm. More intelligent people are also more likely to go crazy. What does that prove? Not much.

Any correlation between faith and education tells us precious little about whether or not God actually exists. If it is true, as Jesus suggests, that the simple and humble see important truths more easily than the learned and the proud (Matthew 11:25), then it would not be surprising for the uneducated to be as wise or wiser in the ways of God than the hypereducated. In the gospel as in *The Emperor's New Clothes*, children see reality more clearly and honestly than pedantic adults. Despite my sixteen years of university education, I am regularly stopped in my tracks by the insights of small children, and the wisdom of men and women whose formal education ended long before mine. Today's educational establishment likes us to believe that because we have more information at our disposal than previous generations, we therefore know more than they did about the meaning of human life. Yet a surfeit of information does not guarantee even a skosh of true wisdom. Common sense often seems to be suffocated in the more-rarefied airs of the academy.

This is not to say that some of the most eminent minds of history have not been religious believers. A brief historical survey suffices to show that religious belief has permeated all social groups, including the intellectuals. Some of the most renowned politicians, historians, artists, scientists, poets, and philosophers have found religious faith to be complementary—not antagonistic—to their professional pursuits.

In my experience, no one caste or worldview has a monopoly on dimwits. I have run into obtuse minds among Christians, Jews, atheists, and Muslims, just as I have known fine minds in all of these categories. I am little impressed by the pseudosophistication of our intellectual elites, with their pretenses of moral superiority. Give me an honest, hardworking man or woman over a self-important academic any day. In the end, the important truths of life are accessible to all, not just to the worldly wise.

Perhaps few of my readers remember June 9, 1982, when Mother Teresa gave her famous address before faculty and students at Harvard University. "How wonderful it is!" she said. "We all long, we all want—even the disbeliever wants—to love God in some way or another. And where is God? How do we love God, whom we don't see? To make it easy for us, to help us to love, He makes himself the hungry one, the naked one, the homeless one."[4] Despite the simplicity of her words, they hit home. She received an overwhelmingly positive response, culminating in a standing ovation. Even the intelligentsia at times have no choice but to acknowledge someone who has grasped real wisdom.

PART II

RELIGION
AND SOCIETY

After having looked at critics' attacks on religion itself, we must turn our attention to the relationship between religion and human society. Many of the atheists' most vehement accusations concern the effects of religion on the public order, and the place of religious believers in the commonwealth. Thus our first order of business will be to examine the atheists' charge that religion is a net evil for society. They allege that, on the whole, our society would be healthier and more secure without religious belief. Contrary to common perception–they add–religion does not make people better. How does this charge stand up to the facts? Does religious belief have a positive effect on people's behavior or not?

One specific area of criticism concerns the relationship between religious belief and war. Pointing to the wars of religion of centuries past as well as to more recent religious disputes, atheists charge that religion is responsible for more deaths than any other single factor. They assure us that even conflicts that are purportedly ethnic or national are in some way religiously motivated. Here we will get to the bottom of these charges. Is there some real tie between violence and religion? Does religion truly encourage people to make war on others, or does it furnish reasons for forgiveness, reconciliation, and love of one's enemies?

Next we will examine the relationship between religion and citizenship. Do religious people make better citizens, or is unbelief a necessary condition of civic virtue? Our atheists charge that religion makes citizens negligent in their duties, since it encourages an unhealthy hope *in a better afterlife. The further we can push religious belief out of the public square—they assert—the stronger and more secure our social cohesion. We will explore the truth of this claim and see how it holds up to the facts.*

A fourth accusation involves believers' alleged desire for the world to end. Christopher Hitchens says that a devout religious person "looks forward to the destruction of the world" and "wishes that end to occur."[1] Is this true? Do believers really seek to expedite the end times? We will hold Hitchens's claims up to the light of Christian belief and practice to see whether they have any justification.

Our next area of exploration is the incrimination of religious parents as guilty of child abuse for teaching their children to believe in God. To expose children to religion can be irreparably damaging, according to our authors. What is to be made of this weighty charge? Are believing parents truly guilty of child abuse and should they have their children removed from their custody? Who should determine what parents may and may not teach their children about life?

We will end this section with a look at believers' rights to share their faith with others. Should we as a society allow religious people to actively announce their beliefs to others? The atheists would like religious people to keep their beliefs to themselves and to leave nonbelievers alone. Is this a reasonable thing to ask? How do we as a society understand the relationship between religion and free speech?

These six charges form the backbone of our upcoming discussion. It is up to you to examine the arguments objectively and arrive at a conclusion.

7.

Does religion do more harm than good?

CHRISTOPHER HITCHENS ASKS WHETHER THE NET effect of religion is positive or negative. Despite the provocative subtitle of his book (*How Religion Poisons Everything*), which seems to imply that religion does nothing but harm, it is reasonable to ask about the real contribution of religion to society.

Rather than examine religious teaching and its effects on society, Hitchens prefers to offer anecdotal evidence for his claim. He begins his thirteenth chapter, titled "Does Religion Make People Behave Better?" with an *ad hominem* attack on Dr. Martin Luther King, Jr. Did King's Christianity make him a better person? Here Hitchens makes a clever, though absurd, assertion. Yes, Martin Luther King, Jr. did all sorts of good things for society in the area of civil rights, but…here's the kicker…he wasn't a Christian. He may have *said* he was a Christian and *thought* he was a Christian, but he was mistaken. "In no real as opposed to nominal sense," Hitchens avers, "was he a Christian."[1] By what rhetorical legerdemain does Hitchens arrive at this conclusion? The only evidence he puts forward to back up this crazy thesis is that King didn't advocate violence and didn't threaten people with hell, so he must not have been a true Christian. This is like saying that Mr. Hitchens couldn't be a *true* atheist, since he is too nice a guy.

So what do atheistic authors make of Christianity's contributions to society? They basically start with the Martin Luther King, Jr. premise: if people did good things, they *couldn't* be religious; if they did bad things, they *must* have been religious—despite the evidence to the contrary. And if evidently religious people did something good, they must have done it *despite* their being religious, and not *because* of it. And so the deck is hopelessly stacked against religion from the start.

Hitchens and company claim to follow the Gospel principle of judging a tree by its fruit, but as for the tree of religion, they consider only the rotten fruit, never the good. The innumerable saints, geniuses, and benefactors given to humanity by the faith, or nourished by it, count for nothing. In making their case, Hitchens and company refrain from considering the almost countless ways that Christianity has benefited the world as we know it today. What of the hospitals? What of the orders of nuns established to care for the dying or to educate young girls? What of the soup kitchens and orphanages? What of the preservation and handing on of classical culture? Instead, they choose to enumerate the things that Christianity *hasn't done* to better the world, or hasn't done well enough, or has simply done too slowly!

This pseudomethodology can be used to discredit anything. Let's take the example of one of the most beneficent disciplines there is: medicine. Imagine if you were to undertake a study of the biggest blunders committed in the name of medicine throughout history—from botched surgeries, to bleeding with leeches, to cranial boring, to the hellish experimentation afflicted by Nazi doctors on war prisoners—and used such research as an indictment of the entire field of medicine. During the unprincipled years of the late nineteenth century, for instance, medical quackery abounded, and hundreds of traveling medicine shows extolled the virtues of worthless potions and products, from Dr. Kilmer's Swamp Root, to Dr. Pierce's Nasal Douche, to Kickapoo Indian Sagwa, to Dr. Hercules Sanche's Oxydonor. By Hitchens's standard, medicine has been an unmitigated disaster for humanity, and all doctors should be shuffled off to the guillotine! Yet, if there can be good medicine and bad medicine, why can't there be good religion and bad religion?

Moreover, in their search for historical examples to make their case, these authors spill very little ink calmly confronting the teachings and practices of religions *today* (except in the case of extreme Islamic fundamentalists) and instead spend page after page describing the most hideous examples they can find of errors committed in the name of religion in centuries past. For example, Pope Benedict XVI and Pope John Paul II before him have repeated over and over again that God and religion cannot be co-opted to justify violence. Violence in the name of religion is an aberration. Yet where does Hitchens acknowledge this?

Time after time Hitchens makes the claim that anything done in the name of religion could just as well be done in the name of secular humanism. Thus, he says, religion really contributes nothing. He seems to miss the more important point. People *actually do* many good things as a result of religious motivation that they wouldn't do otherwise. People *could* be compassionate and selfless in the name of secular humanism, but the fact remains that they more often *are* compassionate and unselfish in the name of religion!

There is no doubt that religious people could do more, and Hitchens's accusations do oblige us to a serious examination of conscience and a renewed commitment to offer a more consistent witness. Yet an impartial examination of the facts will lead any objective observer to the conclusion that religion, and Christianity in particular, has been and continues to be a force for good.

8.

> ## Doesn't religion cause
> ## war and violence?

THE SECOND CHAPTER OF CHRISTOPHER HITCHens's book bears the provocative title "Religion Kills." This is a very serious accusation, and it merits a serious response. Does "religion" kill? Unfortunately, people kill each other all the time. How much of this is religiously motivated? Percentage-wise, not much really. Look at the daily newspapers or watch the evening news. It is a rare thing indeed to hear of a murder committed for religious reasons. How often do you hear of someone pulling a knife on another because they disagree on the doctrine of justification or transubstantiation?

Most killing is motivated by greed, pride, anger,

revenge, and any number of human passions common to the religious and irreligious alike. True, a fair amount of violence is perpetrated between warring bands, and in this regard, affiliation with a given religious sect is no different from affiliation with a tribe or clan or nation. A certain hostility to those outside one's social group is a sad reality of the human condition. Religion is not immune to this phenomenon, but neither is it the cause.

To make a real case, Hitchens would have to show that *religion itself* (again we must ask *which* religion) encourages people to murder and violence. Hitchens and his comrades-in-arms cannot make this case. The fact is that very few people today kill in the name of religion, and fewer still with the *blessings* of religion. Here atheistic authors would do well to acknowledge the important distinction between religious practice and religious *abuse*. For a Christian to kill in the name of Jesus, for instance, is clearly an example of the latter. The moral teachings of Jesus provide no support for—indeed, they stand as a stern rebuke to—the historical crimes perpetrated in the name of Christianity. In this regard Christianity has an internal corrective that atheists do not enjoy. It would be strange indeed for Christians to find justification for their violence in the Prince of Peace!

Though Jesus was no pacifist, He was certainly no warmonger either. He said rather that "all who draw the sword will die by the sword" (Matthew 26:52 NIV). Jesus' teachings regarding forgiveness, love of enemies, and reconciliation fly in the face of Hitchens's claims that religion justifies violence.

Since Hitchens cannot show that religion teaches violence, he instead draws a broad generalization from a few specific examples. He points to historical examples of how ostensibly religious people have killed one another and concludes that religion itself encourages death-dealing. Books such as Hitchens's are chock-full of gruesome anecdotal evidence of how atrocities have been carried out in the name of religion. From bombings in Beirut to massacres in Mumbai, Hitchens and his colleagues spare no detail in chronicling these savageries. Yet here, what do they really prove? No one denies that plenty of evil has been done since the creation (or spontaneous apparition!) of the world, and plenty has been done by purportedly religious people. Does the mere fact that religion can be co-opted for evil purposes mean that religion itself is evil? By that twisted logic, the fact that science has often been put to use for all sorts of devilry (the atomic bomb, chemical weapons... instant coffee) means that science itself must be evil.

Similarly, nationalism has often spawned the greatest atrocities, but does that mean nations should be abolished?

The fact that ethnic and national identities sometimes coincide with religious affiliation doesn't mean that these violent conflicts are always *religious* in nature. There is no need here to nitpick, since surely some of the violence is religiously motivated. Yet we would be disingenuous to accept the claim that every conflict deemed a "religious war" truly had religion at its core. Many of the so-called "wars of religion" were not fought over religion but rather over rival claims to territory and power. The wars between England and France, for instance, can hardly be called religious wars simply because the English were Protestants and the French were Catholics. Ethnic rivalry, not religion, is the core source of the tension in Northern Ireland and the Balkans, not to mention the Middle East. History seems to suggest instead that kinship loyalties, tribal affiliations, and national allegiances—as well as political ideologies—have begotten more violence than any theological debate.

In the Summer 2007 issue of the Claremont Review of Books, Ross Douthat gets it just about right when he examines Christopher Hitchens's astonishing accusation that no atrocity has been committed and no tyranny established that did not somehow have religion at its root. "More likely," writes Douthat, "the reader will come away unpersuaded of anything save the self-evident truth of the matter, which is that human beings, being a clannish and quarrelsome lot, tend to find all sorts of things to fight over, and that nearly every aspect of human affairs can serve as a powerful spur to actions both heroic and deplorable."[1] Amen to that.

Let's be realistic here. The foremost example of religious persecution in America is the Salem witch trials. As terrible as those events were, a total of some twenty-five people were killed as a result.[2] This excuses nothing but does allow for some perspective. The most popular European example of religious villainy is the infamous Spanish Inquisition. The number of people sentenced to death by the Spanish Inquisition—which was active over a period of several hundred years—is estimated at between three thousand and five thousand.[3] Again, no excuses here, but just how long will Christians have to beat their breasts over a tragic historical event they thoroughly condemn? Why continue to indict religion in general, or Christianity in particular, for errors that no one today embraces and that contradict the teachings of its founder?

Now let's compare this to the "gentle" excesses of atheistic slaughter. If we take the century spanning from 1900 to 2000, we discover death tolls in the name of religion-free utopias totaling well over 100 million.[4] That's 100 million human lives arbitrarily snuffed out in the name of a godless paradise. There simply is no point of comparison here. Together, Adolf Hitler, Joseph Stalin, Mao Zedong and Pol Pot produced the kind of mass slaughter that Torquemada couldn't have dreamed of, without even counting the misdeeds of lesser atheistic tyrants. An estimated 61,911,000 were killed in the Soviet Gulag State, 35,236,000 in Communist China, 20,946,000 under National Socialism (Nazism) and 2,035,000 by the Khmer Rouge in Cambodia.[5] The indisputable fact is that all the religions of the world put together have not managed to kill as many people in *all of human history* as have been killed in the name of atheism just in the past few decades. Isn't it about time the atheists issued collective historical apologies for their camp?

9.

Are religious people irresponsible citizens?

FOR CENTURIES THE ENEMIES OF RELIGION HAVE charged that belief in eternal life leads to neglect of the here and now. From Voltaire to Marx, the accusation has been made again and again that an otherworldly focus justifies an insouciant indifference to human civilization. Convinced of the afterlife, atheists charge, believers would be unconcerned with the suffering of their brothers and sisters, and neglectful of their needs.

Recent atheistic authors have been quick to jump on the same hackneyed bandwagon. Yet while they may have the advantage of sound bites on their side, history belies their conclusions. While it may *seem* that belief in eternity would make people less concerned with the fate of their fellow men and women, historically this has not been the case.

Here we must again note the real differences between one religion and another. Some today still advocate a theocracy where the law of the land is identified with God's law. This is the idea behind the Islamic sharia, for instance. In the Western democratic tradition, notably spawned by Christian culture, we understand there to be two separate realms: the secular and the religious. This Christian tradition rejects the idea that religious belief should be the matter of civil law, while insisting that basic morality be encoded in criminal law. Rape, theft, and murder are moral evils condemned by religions, but they also directly threaten public order and the common good.

Atheistic authors suffer from some cognitive dissonance here. On the one hand, they denounce Christians' presence in politics as a danger to the state. They cry out for a thoroughly secular state in which religious belief and religious persons play no part. On the other hand they complain that religious people are blissfully unconcerned with the good of society and civic affairs. Which is it? Too much concern or too little?

The fact is that despite—or because of—their belief in eternity, Christians have good reason for being interested in the welfare of society. While Jesus offered a justification for the separation of church and state, in enjoining his followers to "give to Caesar what is Caesar's, and to God what is God's" (Matthew 22:21 NIV), He did not exempt Christians from their civic duties. In fact, "giving Caesar what is Caesar's" carries with it a series of public responsibilities that Christians cannot take—and historically have not taken—lightly. Christians seek to make society more humane through the passage of laws that respect the true dignity of the human person.

Since the foundation of Christianity, Christians were viewed as a threat to the Roman state, not because of immoral doctrines, but because Christians recognized a parallel (and superior) moral authority to that of the governor. In other words, they questioned the statist absolutism that was commonplace in ancient times and resurrected in the totalitarianisms of the last century. Christians were more than ready to "give to Caesar what is Caesar's," but they were also bound to "give to God what is God's," even if that meant suffering for it by challenging political structures and fighting for true justice.

Let's take a hypothetical situation. Let's say that

you are a typical secular humanist, who believes that God doesn't exist, death ends everything, and man is nothing but a clod of matter slightly more evolved than the snail darter. Maybe you have some natural compassion, so you treat your fellows well—when you feel like it. Other times you don't, since, in the end, you know it really doesn't *matter*. Now let's imagine that you are a Christian. Maybe you aren't naturally empathetic to others and their needs, but you are convinced that after death you will be judged by your deeds and that whatever you do to your least brethren—providing for their material needs, for instance—you do to your Lord (see Matthew 25: 31–46). Which of these two hypothetical persons—Sam the Secularist or Chrissy the Christian—is more likely to reach out to those in need? Which is more likely to work for a more truly human society? You make the call.

10.

Are believers trying to hasten the end of the world?

ONE OF CHRISTOPHER HITCHENS'S MORE PRE-posterous insinuations is that religious peo-ple are dangerous because they want to bring about the end of the world. Give them the reins of society— one infers—and they'll take us by the short road to Armageddon. Not only are believers unafraid of the world ending, they actively would like to bring it about.

This sort of apocalyptic scenario is the stuff of screenplays. You may recall the 1990 film *The Hunt for Red October,* inspired by the Tom Clancy novel of the same name. In it a defecting Soviet subma-rine captain by the name of Marko Ramius (played by Sean Connery) plans to hand over his subma-rine to the United States. Yet he's been reading about Armageddon and it's known that he has been despondent ever since his wife died, so viewers wonder whether he doesn't have something more sinister in mind. This makes for a fine movie script, but it's hardly the story line of a typical religious person.

As is true of so many accusations made by atheists, a cursory look at history suffices to expose Hitchens's prejudices. Have religious heads of state throughout history (remember there have been many!) exhibited this fanatical "let's destroy the world" syndrome? Hitchens doesn't produce a single example. Was that because he couldn't make up his mind which of the many to choose, or rather because *there haven't been any*? Instead, he merely launches his innuendo and drops it at that.

Now I have no doubt that certain deranged minds would like to bring about the end of the world. Psychological disorders come in every shape, size, and color. Yet does this have anything to do with religion? The fact that a madman thinks he is Napoleon, Charles de Gaulle, or Jesus Christ doesn't make his a religious disease. If there were a religion that openly advocated bringing about the end of the world, I agree that it should be opposed. But in invoking examples such as Paul the Apostle and John the Evangelist, Hitchens suggests this may be a trait of Christianity. This is not just demonstrably false—it is absurd.

Hitchens writes that the apostle Paul "hoped that

time was running out for humanity."[1] Of course he offers no citations to back up his claim (there aren't any) so therefore no one will call him on his allegation. A more sophisticated mind would recognize that there is a fundamental difference between *believing* that the world will one day end, *endeavoring to be prepared* for such an eventuality, and *actively working* to bring it about. I cannot speak for all religions, but I can say with absolute assurance that Christianity would unabashedly condemn any attempts to precipitate the destruction of the world.

By analogy we can look at Christians' understanding of their own lives. Christians believe that heaven is better than earth, so there is no reason to fear death. By Hitchens's reasoning, they should therefore be running toward death like a pack of lemmings scurrying to jump off the nearest cliff. Yet that doesn't happen. Unlike atheists, Christians condemn suicide as a grave sin. One thing is to look forward to eternal life *in God's time*; another thing is to expedite its arrival. The former attitude is expected of Christians; the latter is forbidden. Unlike atheists, Christians hold the healthy belief that God is Master of the world and of their lives—not they themselves.

11.

Is religious education a form of child abuse?

ONE OF THE MOST DISTURBING ACCUSATIONS leveled by Harris, Dawkins, and Hitchens in their respective books is that religious education of children is a form of child abuse. Hitchens writes that countless children "had their psychological and physical lives irreparably maimed by the compulsory education of faith."[1] And Richard Dawkins rhetorically asks: "Isn't it always a form of child abuse to label children as possessors of beliefs that they are too young to have thought about?"[2]

This accusation is deeply troubling on several levels.

First, it makes light of real child abuse. While my

seventh-grade religion classes were certainly no picnic, they simply cannot be compared to the real physical and psychological torture suffered by numerous children in the world today. To do so is to callously insult the real sufferings of others. How can the atheists possibly equate religious education with the beatings with electrical cords, sexual assaults, and broken bones that are often the real content of child abuse? I understand that hyperbole is a legitimate literary device, but common decency should impose certain limits.

Second, if Hitchens and company are to be taken literally, religious education should be illegal. Stated bluntly, child abuse is always and everywhere a criminal offense. If teaching children about the existence of a good and loving God is abusive, it should be criminalized as well. In *The God Delusion*, Richard Dawkins writes that he was once asked to comment on publicized cases of child abuse by Catholic priests. He replied that "as horrible as sexual abuse no doubt was, the damage was arguably less than the long-term psychological damage of bringing the child up Catholic in the first place."[3] I find this reasoning downright frightening. By Dawkins's logic, since sexual child abuse is a punishable crime, raising a child Catholic is even more so. Thank God,

Dawkins is teaching at Oxford rather than drafting legislation. Otherwise my dear parents might be sitting behind bars.

Finally, perhaps the scariest element of the child-abuse accusation is the underlying statism of our authors. The only alternative to parent-controlled education is state-controlled education. It has been the general consensus of reasonable people that parents will usually have their children's best interests in mind, more than others who are not their parents. Children nearly always fare better with their parents than with others, and in most civilized societies it takes an egregious act of negligence or abuse to remove a child from the custody of his or her parents—with good reason. The imposition of a homogeneous educational model inculcating radical secularism has already been tried, for instance in the Soviet Union. In case any atheists missed this chapter in our recent history, it didn't go so well.

Who wouldn't like to see his own values and beliefs taught to other people's children? Perhaps most of us—if we are honest—would like to see our own priorities inculcated in the young, convinced that in this way the world would be a much better place. In regard to religion, many Christians would no doubt like to see every child raised Christian, many Jews would no doubt like to see children raised Jewish, and ample literature shows that atheists would like to see all children brought up in a God-free world. Yet this isn't the way things are. To propose an educational power play smacks of totalitarianism. We really don't want to go there. Some parents teach their children downright wacky things, yet this is unavoidable. Freedom is sacred within due limits—and that includes parental freedom. True child abuse extends beyond those due limits; sincere religious belief in a loving God does not.

Hitchens's censuring of religious education extends to training in morality as well, especially when it conflicts with the censurer's particular morality. A bizarre example of Hitchens's understanding of "child abuse" is teaching one's children that abortion is morally wrong. Hitchens advocates abortion as a form of birth control when other methods have failed (he calls abortion a "fallback solution") and feels that others should see things the way he does.[4] So where he has no problem with parents teaching their children that it is right to recycle and wrong to smoke cigarettes, he sees moral instruction about abortion as child abuse. One begins to see a pattern here. Any parent who doesn't instill Hitchens's peculiar worldview is abusive.

It is possible to teach any good lesson in an overly draconian manner, and the result is often the contrary to what is hoped for and intended. A child who is never allowed to spend a dime may rebel upon growing into independence and become a profligate adult. Children confined at home may later become wanderers. Unfortunately this occurs at times with religion as well; children who grow up receiving a religious message in a strictly negative light often reject it. But in the case of religion, the tragedy of such an upbringing is doubly poignant: the child not only grows up repressed and unhappy, but he or she may also reject ultimate fulfillment in a relationship with God—due solely to an unloving educational approach.

I would like to close this section with a personal story. Five years ago I became friends with a young woman named Carol who had grown up in a God-less home. Her parents were part of the sixties generation that believed children should "make up their own minds" about God, rather than being indoctrinated in the faith of their parents. Naturally, being nonbelievers themselves, Carol's parents made no effort to pass along religious faith.

When Carol was in her early twenties, she started investigating the Christian faith that her parents had rejected. She felt envious of her friends who had received some sort of catechesis and knew the basics of their faith better than she did. The expression she used struck me very hard at the time. Carol said she felt she had been "cheated" by her parents, because they had given her no faith. All those years when she could have been believing, she remained ignorant of God because her parents hadn't taught her. Now she was determined to make up for lost time.

Is it more "abusive" for parents to share their faith with their children, or to withhold it from them?

12.

Should believers be allowed to proselytize?

THE ATHEISTS RESENT BELIEVERS' ATTEMPTS TO convince others of God's existence. In *God Is Not Great,* Christopher Hitchens asserts that all he wants is that religious people *"leave me alone."* Yet this appears to be impossible. Hitchens writes that religion *"must* seek to interfere with the lives of unbelievers." He says that the true believer "cannot rest until the whole world bows the knee" and even avers that for the pious, those who decline to recognize religious authority "have forfeited their right to exist."[1] This crescendo of accusations focuses especially on believers' insistence on trying to share their beliefs with others and to convince them of their truth.

Allow me to ask a pointed question here. Why did Christopher Hitchens write *God Is Not Great*? Was it not to convince readers that God does not exist? Doesn't Hitchens seek to interfere with the lives of believers? Doesn't he want the whole world to share in his enlightened state? Hitchens claims that all he wants from religious believers is reciprocity, which for him means to be left alone. Yet one cannot help but wonder how penning a three-hundred-page screed against religion can be qualified as leaving believers alone. The impression readers are left with after reading his work is that Mr. Hitchens is as zealous in his atheist proselytism as the fieriest Bible-thumper is in his. Why should the rights of believers to express their worldview be any less than the rights of Christopher Hitchens to express his?

But let's stop for a moment to ask ourselves why believers—and again, I speak here primarily of Christians—seek to win over adherents, or *evangelize*. Is it, as Hitchens claims, because of the compulsive nature of religion to propagate itself? Or could there be a *reasonable* and even *noble* motive for wanting to spread one's faith? Some may, indeed, do so out of ignoble motives. Some may simply want to swell the ranks of their particular tribe or sect. Yet in my experience a great many do so in the sincere conviction that they are sharing something wonderful, a treasure. They are passing on a message that changed their lives for the better. They believe that in sharing their faith, they are giving a gift.

If you were to discover a cure for cancer or AIDS, what would be your first order of business? You would undoubtedly communicate this find to the medical world so that the greatest number of people could avail themselves of the cure as soon as possible. You would want the results published in a medical journal and announced on television. You would, in fact, be negligent not to do so. Now Christians are convinced that they have received not just a remedy for cancer, but an overwhelming truth of eternal proportions: God loves us and sent His only Son to be our Redeemer. To fail to pass on that truth would be criminally negligent!

I intensely disagree with Christopher Hitchens's basic message, but I heartily support his right to voice his opinions. Thankfully, our democratic, Judeo-Christian civilization invites us to treat others with respect, even when we disagree with them. Though I may disagree with the Jehovah's Witnesses that come every so often knocking at my door, I am not for that reason entitled to drive them away with a stick. As a society, we believe in peaceful discourse, and every person's right to self-expression, within reasonable bounds. One wonders why Hitchens would want to deprive religious people of the very rights they extend to him.

In an interview on CNBC in October 2007, Christian writer Ann Coulter dared to say that she thought the world would be a better place if everyone were Christian. She also said she believes that Jews who accept Jesus as their Savior are "perfected."[2] She was immediately deluged with a veritable firestorm of criticisms, some bordering on the hysterical. Abe Foxman, director of the Anti-Defamation League, labeled Coulter anti-Semitic,[3] and others went so far as to argue that her words will lead to another Auschwitz. Paradoxically, it was Dennis Prager, a Jewish writer and lecturer, who immediately came to Coulter's defense. His words bear repeating here:

> As a practicing Jew, I do not agree with Ann Coulter's theology any more than those attacking her do. But I am neither offended by her nor frightened by her or her beliefs. She believes that Christianity is better than Judaism. So what? Why is that in any way different from liberals thinking that liberalism is truer and morally superior to conservatism? Or conservatives thinking that their values are superior to liberal values?

Liberals not only believe that conservatives are philosophically imperfect, but they often believe that conservatives are bad human beings....Liberals yearn for a world without conservatives at least as much as most believing Christians want a world without non-Christians. The difference is many liberals are immeasurably more likely to impose their views on others than Christian Americans are.[4]

This is what scares me most about the proposals of Hitchens and his clan. Civil disagreement is part and parcel of the free society. As long as it is done peacefully and respectfully, public discourse on significant topics—such as religion—forms an important column of the democratic system. Outlawing free speech when we disagree with others' opinions, on the other hand, is the mark of totalitarianism. Who is the dangerous one here?

PART III

Faith—Science— Reason

One of the most common objections to religious belief today is its supposed incompatibility with scientific knowledge. The age of science was supposed to replace the age of religion, since it provided a better explanation of the natural world that we live in. We no longer "need" God—the theory goes—since now we really know how things are. Moreover, religion would be irrational, based on ignorance rather than evidence.

We will break this objection into parts to respond in a more comprehensive way. First we will look at the claim that science has disproved God's existence. In the name of science and *reason our authors express dogmatic certainty regarding God's nonexistence. How did they arrive at this absolute assurance? Has science driven the final nail into religion's coffin, or is atheistic certainty itself a form of irrational belief?*

Next we will examine the atheists' criticism that the Bible utterly misrepresents the origins of the world and humanity. According to Hitchens, Dawkins, and Harris, science has demonstrated the falsity of a Christian understanding of Creation, so one can embrace it only by closing one's eyes to scientific fact. What exactly does the Bible tell us about where we come from? Does it contradict the findings of paleontology and evolutionary biology? Must one choose between biblical belief and science, or are they in some way compatible?

This discussion leads us to the next objection posed by the atheists: Christianity is hostile to science. According to these authors, Christianity has always sought to stifle scientific inquiry because it represents a competing explanation of reality. Religion is a power game, so keeping people in ignorance is necessary to exert authority over people's lives. How does this accusation stand up to historical fact? Is Christianity inimical to science? Are the two mutually exclusive?

The atheists also assure us that since science is incompatible with religion, all true scientists are atheists, or at least agnostics. One cannot maintain a scientific worldview in the laboratory—they say—without first sloughing off a religious worldview. What do the facts reveal in this case? Are all scientists atheists? Or if some persist in their belief, do they find themselves living immersed in contradictions?

Finally, we will examine the atheists' claim that religious faith is simply irrational. According to several authors, atheism is the only reasonable choice, since it alone respects the findings of honest, impartial inquiry into the facts, without being bound by doctrines and dogmas. Here we will inquire whether religious faith means tossing reason out the window, or whether faith and reason work together in harmony. Does religious belief suffocate reason, or does faith enrich and complete our empirical knowledge of the world? These are the questions to be answered. Let's get to it!

13.

A DISTINCTIVE CHARACTERISTIC OF ATHEISTIC writers is their dogmatic certainty that God doesn't exist. They intentionally distance themselves from agnostics who merely *doubt* the existence of God and plant themselves firmly in the camp of anti-theistic certitude. Thus, though Richard Dawkins expresses unqualified openness to nearly *everything*, including the existence of other universes and intelligent life elsewhere within our own, he exhibits nothing but the most intransigent assurance regarding God's nonexistence. Dawkins, Hitchens, Dennett, and Harris all share the conviction that the "God hypothesis" has been laid to rest, once and for all.

From these atheists' unshakable certainty, one would assume they had discovered incontrovertible proof that God is a fake. Is this the case? Has there been some scientific breakthrough that demonstrates God doesn't exist? Has someone discovered a "God gene" that causes a collective fantasy of God's existence? Of course not. The bravado of atheists' rhetoric is completely disproportionate to the poverty of their "scientific" arguments for God's nonexistence. So despite their contention that we can now know, with finality and certainty, that God does not exist and that organized religion is a fraud, the fact remains that their major arguments attacking God's existence fall as flat as a yeast-free pancake.

The most serious attempt to disprove God's existence comes from evolutionary biologist Richard Dawkins. To accomplish this herculean task, Dawkins converts the God question into a matter for science. One of the sharpest criticisms that Dawkins received uniformly from reviewers—believers and nonbelievers alike—concerned his reckless foray into an area completely outside his competence. Rather than write about evolutionary biology, with which he surely possesses some degree of familiarity, he chose to write about religion, all the while pretending he was writing about science.

And so in musing about God's existence, Dawkins states: "Either he exists or he doesn't. It is a scientific question." He adds that "the presence or absence of a creative super-intelligence is univocally a scientific question."[1]

Dawkins has as much right as anyone to express his opinions regarding God's existence. The problem is that he insists on speaking as a *scientist*, as if that gives him some special competence in answering religious questions. Unfortunately for Dawkins, science has nothing whatever to say regarding the existence of spiritual realities. Dawkins tries to get over this rather formidable obstacle by whittling God down to a size that science can handle. Being a convinced materialist, Dawkins rules out *a priori* the existence of nonmaterial entities. In order to exist—Dawkins surmises—God must conform to the laws of the universe like any other natural entity. Therefore, He can be observed. Dawkins treats God as if He were a measurable phenomenon like light refraction or the Doppler effect. And so he logically concludes that "the God question is not in principle and forever outside the remit of science."[2]

In the end, Dawkins's "scientific" explanation for God's nonexistence rests on an argument of probability. Since he rightly recognizes that science cannot *disprove* the existence of anything, he relies on statistical improbability, the "big one," as he calls it, toward which all his other arguments converge. His conclusions turn out to be deeply disappointing, however, especially after the buildup he provides for them. Though he offers a veneer of scientific underpinnings for his argument, it ends up being a simple philosophical fallacy.

Dawkins's argument reads like this: "However statistically improbable the entity you seek to explain by invoking a designer, the designer himself has got to be at least as improbable."[3] In other words, since the Creator would always have to be superior to—more complex and intelligent than—His creation, God will always be more unlikely than even the most complex, improbable creature. There would thus be a scale of complexity of beings, at the top of which we would find God.

It takes but little thought to realize that one cannot speak about God's *probability*, since probability always refers to contingent beings and God is posited as a necessary Being. Probability refers to the relative possibility that an event will occur, as expressed by the ratio of the number of *actual* occurrences to the total number of *possible* occurrences. Something is probable or improbable according to the statistical regularity of its occurrence. God doesn't work that way. He is not an event that "comes about" after a wildly improbable alignment of causal conditions. God is understood to be essentially distinct from, prior to, and superior to the created world. God either exists or He doesn't, but probability has nothing to do with it.

Where the notion of probability can legitimately be used is in calculating the likelihood of phenomena such as the appearance of life on Earth. In these cases one can evaluate the prospect of all the necessary conditions to be simultaneously present. This works for any natural event and can be used up to a point to indicate the relative necessity of intervention from outside a given natural system, i.e., God. Where it decidedly doesn't work is in gauging the likelihood of the existence of a supernatural being.

The underlying problem is that Dawkins's God is not what Christians understand by "God." Dawkins creates a straw man—or straw *divinity*—to his own measure, and then disproves his existence. The supernatural Being that Christians call *God* is necessarily beyond the reach of the empirical sciences, since He is not a lump of matter or an energy force. He cannot be the object of observation and experimentation that the hard sciences require. To debate God's existence, we must at the very least agree on what we mean by "God." Atheists propose a god that is unrecognizable to religious believers.

14.

> ## Doesn't the Bible misrepresent the origins of man and the cosmos?

A S WE HAVE SEEN, EARLY ON IN *GOD IS NOT GREAT,* Christopher Hitchens lays out his four "irreducible objections" to religious faith, the first of which is that "it wholly misrepresents the origins of man and the cosmos."[1] Sam Harris latches onto the same argument and excoriates Christians who "believe that the entire cosmos was created six thousand years ago...about a thousand years after the Sumerians invented glue."[2]

While strict creationists do hold to some rather far-fetched opinions regarding the origins of the world, most Christians reject a literal reading of the Genesis account of God's creation of the world in six

24-hour days. There is no official Christian doctrine concerning the exact way that creation came about, though we do universally believe in "God, the Father Almighty, Creator of heaven and earth." The book of Genesis teaches us many important lessons concerning God, His relationship with human beings, and the meaning of human existence. Few today believe, however, that Genesis intends to present a historically accurate play-by-play account of the first hours of the world. Even fundamentalists recognize the problem with three full "days" going by before the creation of the sun.

Scientists seem to agree that the universe is approximately 14 billion years old, and the earth appears to be some 4.5 billion years old. I cannot verify that, but neither do I have a problem with it. Furthermore, the scientific community has nearly unanimously accepted the theory of the Big Bang as the best explanation we currently possess regarding the origins of the universe. I am not a scientist, so my opinion of the Big Bang carries very little weight, but what does seem evident to me is that (1) interpretations of the Big Bang vary widely, and (2) there is no fundamental incompatibility between the Big Bang and a biblical discussion of the origins of the universe.

So whereas Christopher Hitchens decries religion, and especially Christianity, as misrepresenting the origins of man and the cosmos, others—even within the scientific community—heartily disagree. Francis S. Collins, the leader of the monumental Human Genome Project, offers another interpretation of the origins of the universe. "The Big Bang cries out for a divine explanation. It forces the conclusion that nature had a defined beginning. I cannot see how nature could have created itself. Only a supernatural force outside of space and time could have done that."[3] In other words, the Big Bang itself needs a cause.

In his book *God and the Astronomers*, astrophysicist Robert Jastrow wrote that "the astronomical and biblical accounts of Genesis are the same; the chain of events leading to man commenced suddenly and sharply at a definite moment in time, in a flash of light and energy."[4] And the Nobel Prize–winning scientist Arno Penzias, who co-discovered the cosmic microwave background radiation that lent strong support to the Big Bang, said: "The best data we have are exactly what I would have predicted, had I nothing to go on but the five books of Moses, the Psalms, the Bible as a whole."[5]

Whereas near unanimity reigns in the scientific

community regarding the origins of the universe, science currently has much less to offer concerning the origins of life. Thus while Richard Dawkins's explanation of biological development is quite plausible as far as it goes, it does nothing to explain the origins of life itself, without which biological evolution is impossible. Natural selection, in fact, presupposes life but does nothing to explain the genesis of life, nor its statistical improbability. It seeks only to explain the survival and gradual change of reproducing species. Thus the following quotation cited by Dawkins himself retains all its relevance: "Hoyle said that the probability of life originating on earth is no greater than the chance that a hurricane, sweeping through a scrapyard, would have the luck to assemble a Boeing 747."[6]

Again, I would have no problem with science offering an explanation for the origins of life, and this would not harm my Christian faith in any way. I am only saying that this has not yet been done and may never be done, for all I know. Collins writes that "no current hypothesis comes close to explaining how in the space of a mere 150 million years, the prebiotic environment that existed on earth gave rise to life."[7]

To get over this formidable hump, Dawkins has

recourse to the anthropic principle to explain the origins of life. This principle is substantially less convincing than natural selection and ends up explaining very little. The anthropic principle basically says that our universe is uniquely tuned to give rise to human life. In Dawkins's words: "There are billions of planets in the universe, and, however small the minority of evolution-friendly planets may be, our planet necessarily has to be one of them." He goes on to say that at the cosmological level, "it follows from the fact of our existence that the laws of physics must be friendly enough to allow life to arise."[8] These statements are, of course, self-evidently true but *explain* exactly nothing. Dawkins can interpret this as a sign that God doesn't exist (though it's not clear how), and others, like scientist Stephen Hawking, can read the exact opposite meaning into the facts. In *A Brief History of Time*, Hawking states: "It would be very difficult to explain why the universe should have begun in just this way, except as the act of a God who intended to create beings like us."[9]

I do not know how God brought about the universe, nor how He created human life. Christians should, and do, encourage scientists in their continuing endeavor to find out. Christians have no horse in this race. What we do believe is that at the origin of all that is, we find God and His Son, Jesus Christ. "All things came into being through him, and without him not one thing came into being" (John 1:3). Where Christians see compatibility, neo-atheists insist on seeing enmity.

15.

Is Christianity against science?

RELIGION IS "AN ENEMY OF SCIENCE AND INQUIRY," writes Christopher Hitchens.[1] The logic behind his accusation runs like this: Religion hates science, because religion is about power. Once people learn how nature really works, they won't need God anymore and they won't need churches or church leaders to tell them what to do. Church leaders will lose their influence and power, so they cannot let that happen. Therefore, church leaders will always try to thwart science.

Richard Dawkins, for instance, writes: "Mystics exult in mystery and want it to stay mysterious...One of the truly bad effects of religion is that it teaches us that it is a virtue to be satisfied with not under-standing."[2] Both Dawkins and Hitchens declare that religion is inimical to science. Science and religion cannot peacefully coexist—they say—since they offer contrary explanations of reality. Since only one can survive, one must go, and the two are in a fight to the death.

The example to be trotted out is always, of course, the case of the seventeenth-century mathematician and astronomer Galileo Galilei. Though the case was hardly a molehill, it wasn't nearly the moun-tain it has been made to become. Real errors were made—scientific, theological, and moral—and injus-tices committed, and no one today disagrees with this. Still, opposition to aspects of the work of one scientist in one isolated period (Isn't it interesting how Galileo is—across the board—the only example cited by the opposition? One would think they could list a whole slew of examples if their argument had weight...) hardly disqualifies the unhesitating sup-port that Christian churches have given to the natu-ral sciences over the course of two millennia.

Religion's supposed hostility to learning extends to other disciplines as well. Christopher Hitchens writes, "The attitude of religion to medicine, like the attitude of religion to science, is always problematic and very often necessarily hostile." He adds that medical research only began to flourish once "the priests had been elbowed aside."[3] Strangely, in the very next line he quotes Louis Pasteur as an example of this enlightened research, without acknowledging that Pasteur was a pious Catholic Christian!

Before getting to theory, perhaps we should look at the facts that belie this charge. The first simple fact is that the natural sciences grew out of Christian culture. As the sociologist Rodney Stark has so convincingly shown, science was "still-born" in the great civilizations of the ancient world, *except* in Christian civilization.[4] Why is it that empirical science and the scientific method did not develop in China (with its sophisticated society), in India (with its philosophical schools), in Arabia (with its advanced mathematics), in Japan (with its dedicated craftsmen and technologies), or even in ancient Greece or Rome?

The answer is fairly straightforward. Science flourished in societies where a Christian mind-set understood nature to be ordered and intelligible, the work of an intelligent Creator. Science grew where people assumed that the natural world is intelligible and bears the handwriting of its Author. Far from being an obstacle to science, Christian soil was the necessary humus where science took root.

Christianity's unapologetic support of science is borne out by the immense direct contribution of the Christian Church to science itself. To take but one area—that of astronomy—J. L. Heilbron of the University of California, Berkeley has written: "The Roman Catholic Church gave more financial aid and social support to the study of astronomy for over six centuries, from the recovery of ancient learning during the late Middle Ages into the Enlightenment, than any other, and, probably, all other, institutions."[5]

With this in mind, Christopher Hitchens's claim that "the right to look through telescopes and speculate about the result was obstructed by the church"[6] is especially puzzling.

What can be said of astronomy can be said equally of medicine, physics, mathematics, and chemistry. Just as the Christian Church patronized the arts, so it vigorously supported scientific research. The caricature of an obscurantist, ignorance-promoting church simply doesn't correspond to historical truth. Some of history's greatest scientists—Newton, Pasteur, Galilei, Lavoisier, Kepler, Copernicus, Faraday, Maxwell, Bernard, and Heisenberg—were all Christians, and the list doesn't stop there.

One small piece of the atheists' accusations is true, however. Religion stands firmly against an absolutist reading of science. Religion—Christianity in particular—staunchly refuses to grant the empirical sciences a monopoly on knowledge and truth. Scientific knowledge is not the only real knowledge, no matter what the atheists may say. Dawkins, for instance, confuses "scientific questions" with questions of fact in general and thereby arrogates to science the entire sphere of the factual. According to Dawkins, whenever a question can be answered yes or no, it must therefore be a question for science. This simply isn't the case. As important as science is, it clearly cannot do everything, and a modicum of scientific modesty—the simple acknowledgment of the boundaries of the field—would be most refreshing. Mathematics, for instance, answers questions that science cannot. Philosophy, too, explores regions beyond the reach of empirical observation. And religion as well tackles questions outside the competence of scientific study.

Whereas Dawkins asserts that any significant question is a scientific question, in reality many important questions—the most important, really—fall outside the purview of science. *What is the meaning of life? How should people treat one another? What happens to us when we die?* No matter how long a white-coated scientist toils and sweats in his laboratory, his instruments will never reveal the answers to these questions. Science is the wrong tool for the job. You cannot scale Mount Everest by using a microscope and scalpel. You cannot navigate the Pacific Ocean with a vernier caliper. You cannot answer life's ultimate questions through scientific investigation.

A scientific hubris that denies the competence of both religion and other disciplines to make truth claims doesn't do much to advance the needed dialogue between religion and science. Then again, maybe these atheists don't want to encourage this dialogue. Hitchens does write, after all, that "all attempts to reconcile faith with science and reason are consigned to failure and ridicule."[7] If this is the foreordained conclusion, there is no sense continuing to dialogue. But then who is being closed-minded here—religion or "science"?

16.

Aren't all scientists and thinking people atheists, or at least agnostics?

RICHARD DAWKINS TAKES GREAT PAINS TO SHOW that Einstein's belief in God was really not belief in a personal God, but in some other cosmic force. He seems to feel it is important to enlist the support of not only Einstein, but any number of contemporary scientists to show that just as real men don't eat quiche, real scientists don't believe in God. Christopher Hitchens, too, suggests that no legitimate scientist could believe in the biblical God, since religion is "an enemy of science and inquiry."[1]

It's important to remember that scientists possess no special insight into God. Science today holds an exaggerated importance, such that we attach a quasi-sacred authority to everything expressed in the name of science. We assume that scientists are smart, educated, circumspect, and objective in their judgment. This may sometimes be true, but scientists are also human beings, specialized in a determined area of human knowledge, and possess no particular credibility or expertise in areas outside their own.

The highly articulate neuroscientist Maureen Condic, of the University of Utah, illustrated the relationship between science and ethics with colorful, provocative, and refreshingly honest comments:

> Scientists are human beings and we are all striving in our own way to reconcile our personal beliefs with our profession, what we do and why we do it. And yet my personal opinion about the morality or immorality of what I do is simply that: It is not a scientific position.
>
> To ask a scientist what their position is and then to credit that position with some dignity due to the fact that the person is a scientist is misleading.
>
> We put up scientific experts and say, "Well, because you've won the Nobel Prize, what is your moral feeling?" But the reality is that winning the Nobel Prize does not mean that the person has any particular capacity to evaluate the moral dimension of his or her work.[2]

For the sake of argument, however, let's look for a moment at how the greatest scientists of all time stood up to the God question. According to the studies of John Galbraith Simmons, of the top twenty scientists in history, fifteen were religious believers (four of whom were deists), two were agnostic, and three were atheists.[3] There were more Catholics among them (five) than either agnostics or atheists, and five more came from other Christian denominations. Thus a full half of the most influential scientists in history were Christians. Again, this says little about the truth claims of Christianity, but it does dispel the myth that good scientists must be atheists.

Sir Isaac Newton, for instance, whom Simmons considers to be the most important scientist who ever lived, was aided greatly in his scientific endeavors by his belief in an ordered universe created by a God of order. Thus he could write, "It is the perfection of God's works that they are all done with the greatest simplicity. He is the God of order and not of confusion."[4] He saw no incompatibility between his Christian faith and the purity of his science, as one complemented the other. "In the absence of any other proof, the thumb alone would convince me of God's existence."[5]

The great French scientist Louis Pasteur, number

five on Simmons's list, was a devout Catholic Christian as well as the developer of the germ theory of disease and the process of "pasteurization." He was able to wed an endearing humility and rich faith to scientific genius. "I have the faith of a Breton peasant," he said later in life, "and by the time I die I hope to have the faith of a Breton peasant's wife."[6]

The late Stephen Jay Gould himself, whom Christopher Hitchens refers to as a "great paleontologist,"[7] threw a monkey wrench in the atheist works by asserting the compatibility of faith and science. Remarking on surveys showing that half of all scientists are religious, Gould commented amusingly that "either half my colleagues are enormously stupid, or else the science of Darwinism is fully compatible with conventional religious beliefs—and equally compatible with atheism."[8]

All in all, some 40 percent of professional scientists claim to believe in God, according to a 1997 study.[9] This varied little during a period of eighty-plus years, since a 1914 study had shown that 41 percent of the scientific community believed in God at the time.[10] Again, God's existence is not a derivative of opinion polls, and 100 percent belief would not produce a God who did not exist, any more than 100 percent atheism would destroy Him if He did.

What these figures do show is that belief in God is not incompatible with serious science.

For many scientists, religious faith is an essential part of life. Other scientists reject the idea of God and prefer to carry on with their lives as if He did not exist. "Science" as such, however, has no position whatever regarding God's existence. The difference between belief and nonbelief is not a difference between rational and irrational, or smart and stupid, but often reflects a deeper willingness or unwillingness to venture into a domain where we do not hold all the cards in our hands.

17.

Is religious faith irrational?

IN *GOD IS NOT GREAT*, CHRISTOPHER HITCHENS asserts that whereas religion depends "upon ignorance and superstition," he and his atheist colleagues respect "free inquiry, openmindedness, and the pursuit of ideas for their own sake."[1] He paints religion as an irrational embrace of ridiculous superstitions, as opposed to atheists' objective, patient sifting through of ideas. As it turns out, however, neither of these caricatures does justice to reality.

Let's first look at faith and reason. Is it true that religion depends on ignorance? Is religious belief incompatible with reason? Hitchens claims that "to believe in a god is in one way to express a *willing-*

ness to believe in anything."[2] This is not true. Faith is not an expression of puerile credulity. Many people arrive at belief in God after careful study and analysis. After pondering different proposals concerning the nature of the world and the meaning of life, many come to the reasoned conclusion that religious faith offers a better explanation for reality than materialistic accounts. It is true that often people spontaneously assume the religion of their parents or surrounding culture. Still, many times people have to compare their beliefs with their personal experience and other belief systems, and must weigh arguments for and against. In this way a more naive faith comes little by little to a deeper maturity.

I am a Catholic Christian. I find the teachings of Jesus Christ to be compelling, and I believe that He is who He claimed to be. The proposal He offers regarding the nature of God and the meaning of human existence finds an echo in my own experience and explains many facets of human life that otherwise seem dark and senseless. My belief reflects not a blind leap of faith but entails the daily engagement of my reason. I am happy to listen to criticism, and to hold others' objections up to my own worldview for comparison. True religion, in my experience, does not contradict reason or suspend rationality. It depends on them.

There have been a number of attempts throughout history to prove the existence of God. Thomas Aquinas is credited with the most celebrated effort at showing God's existence, with his five "ways" or proofs of the existence of God.[3] Philosophers and theologians have labored over and debated about these arguments for centuries, and entire books have been dedicated to discussing their merits, yet our atheist authors quickly dismiss them as unworthy of serious consideration. Richard Dawkins, for instance, discards Aquinas's five ways after a mere three pages, concluding that they are "easily... exposed as vacuous."[4] No matter what you make of the convincing power of these proposals, one thing they are certainly not is "vacuous," and this judgment is as superficial as it is insulting to the generations of eminent thinkers who have discussed these theses in great depth.

Rather than an enemy of reason, religion has often been reason's greatest ally. Christianity in particular affirms the importance of reason and its ability to grasp the truth. In the face of a modern tendency to accentuate the limitations and conditions of human reason, Christianity has often come to the defense of reason. Thus the biblical author writes: "Blessed is the man who meditates on wisdom and who reasons intelligently. He who reflects in his mind on her ways will also ponder her secrets" (Sirach 14:20–21 RSV). A faith devoid of reason degenerates into fideism and exposes itself to errors of every sort.

At the same time, if reason remains closed to faith and refuses to acknowledge that anything can be known beyond the limits of itself, then it stunts its true purpose. Reason devoid of faith easily degenerates into a sort of circular, self-cannibalizing rationalism. While faith never contradicts reason, it surpasses it. Christians believe that there is a profound and indissoluble unity between the knowledge of reason and the knowledge of faith, since truth is one. Rather than compete with each other, reason and faith complement and complete one another. It is in this light that the great Pope John Paul II could write in 1998: "Faith therefore has no fear of reason, but seeks it out and has trust in it. Just as grace builds on nature and brings it to fulfillment, so faith builds upon and perfects reason."[5]

Having looked at the relationship between faith and reason, let's now address the second claim: that atheists rely solely on reason and fact and are therefore exempt from dogmatism. Hitchens insists: "Our belief is not a belief. Our principles are not a faith," and adds, "We do not hold our convictions dogmatically."[6] Richard Dawkins concurs with Hitchens: "Atheists do not have faith."[7] Yet these declarations deserve more than a little skepticism. In reading through their texts, I have encountered as much or more dogmatism as in any of Cotton Mather's sermons.

We must get one thing clear from the start: atheism involves a *choice* just as theism does. The exclusion of God is not the only possible reading of the facts, and reason does not compel a thinking person to deny God's existence. Just as religious faith involves not only the reason but also the will, so, too, does the decision not to believe. Atheism evidences a *refusal* to admit the possibility of God's existence. A simple analysis of the facts cannot compel a person to belief or unbelief. A choice must be made. But it is disingenuous for the atheists to assert that their choice is based simply on fact.

When Dawkins insists that atheists do not have faith, one assumes he means that atheists take nothing on say-so, but rather demand empirical proof for everything. This is false. The atheists hold certain preconceived notions regarding reality by which they interpret the information at their disposal.

Chief among these is their materialism. Material-ism, we must remember, is a worldview, a faith (if you will), and *not* a scientific discovery. To systematically exclude the possibility that anything exists beyond matter and energy constitutes a philosophical belief system all its own, and there is nothing "scientific" about it.

On closer analysis, in fact, one readily sees that Richard Dawkins exhibits a boundless faith in the power of science to heal all ills and answer all questions. It really is quite moving to see someone with such unabashed and uncritical enthusiasm for his own field. He rhetorically queries that "if science cannot answer some ultimate question, what makes anybody think that religion can?"[8] Such fundamen-talism deserves the same answer as the question "If the Bible cannot answer a certain question, what makes anyone think that science can?"

I would challenge these atheistic authors to make good on their offer of open-mindedness. The dog-matic elimination of the possibility of God's existence makes a poor case for atheistic reasonableness.

PART IV

CHRISTIANITY UNDER FIRE

T*hough atheistic authors take issue with God Himself and religion in general, they devote dozens of pages to criticizing Christianity in particular. They attack the foundations of Christianity as well as its doctrines, in an attempt to undermine both its historical roots and its internal consistency. In this section we will address these issues, breaking them into the following topics.*

First, we will look at God Himself, as presented by the biblical authors. How does Sacred Scripture portray God? Does He come across as the "malevolent bully" that atheist Richard Dawkins sees, or rather as a just and loving

Father, faithful to His promises? If the biblical God is truly "the most unpleasant character in all fiction" (to quote Dawkins once again),[1] how is it that He has been able to capture the love and devotion of Christians down through the ages? Is there more to this question than meets the eye?

The atheists' second objection relates to the historicity of Jesus Christ. Did Jesus actually exist, or is He an invention of a group of unscrupulous hucksters who sought to create a religion around a myth of their own creation? Atheistic authors question not only the teachings of Jesus, but His very existence as a man who walked the earth. How does their claim stand up to the historical record? What evidence actually exists to back up Christians' belief in Jesus?

Next we must turn to the historical value of the New Testament. The four Gospels clearly attest to the existence of Jesus, but are they admissible as historical documents? Do they convey an accurate picture of the life and death, words and deeds of Jesus of Nazareth? The atheistic authors naturally assert that the Gospel accounts are worthless as historical texts, because of their internal inconsistencies and stated intent to promote faith in Jesus. How do the documents actually measure up as historical texts? Are they a reliable source of information about Jesus?

Another of the atheists' accusations concerns the Christian Church. They claim that even if Jesus did exist, He never intended to found a church. This latter innovation would be the work of the generations that came after Him and twisted His original intention. Again, our task here will be to inquire after the historical record. Do we have any reason to believe that the founding of a visible community of believers played a part in Jesus' mission on earth? Did Jesus intend to establish a church or didn't He?

Finally, we will examine a very specific criticism regarding Christians' attitudes toward sex. Christopher Hitchens attributes special weight to this topic, which for him constitutes one of the "four irreducible objections to religious faith." Is there any merit to Hitchens's claim that religious faith causes sexual repression? Do Christians indeed hate sex, as the atheists allege? This is a serious accusation that deserves a thoughtful response.

These, then, are the subjects to be covered in this section. How does Christianity stand up to the wave of criticisms leveled by the atheists? Let's take a look.

18.

Is the God of the Bible
a jealous sadist?

NONE OF THE ATHEISTIC AUTHORS HAVE ANY-
thing nice to say about God, which is to be
expected. As I said in the introduction, a reader rap-
idly perceives that the atheists are anything but indif-
ferent to God. It is not an overstatement to say that
they despise Him. Richard Dawkins's description of
God deserves to be quoted in full. Alert readers may
notice that Dawkins permits himself to stray slightly
from the objective, antiseptic language we have come
to expect from the scientific community:

> The God of the Old Testament is arguably the most
> unpleasant character in all fiction: jealous and proud
> of it; a petty, unjust, unforgiving control-freak; a

vindictive, bloodthirsty ethnic cleanser; a misogynistic, homophobic, racist, infanticidal, genocidal, filicidal, pestilential, megalomaniacal, sadomasochistic, capriciously malevolent bully.[1]

The ethnic cleansing and sadomasochism are one thing, but a control freak? Come on! Dawkins peppers his treatise with further divine name-calling. The biblical God is "interventionist, miracle-wreaking, thought-reading, sin-punishing, prayer-answering," a "psychotic delinquent," and a "monster."[2]

Now some of this hardly sounds like a serious indictment, except for the obviously derogatory tone in which it is written. Other than the last two elements, it almost sounds like attributes that belong on a Father's Day card! "Interventionist" could be reexpressed as caring, "sin-punishing" as just, and "thought-reading" as sensitive. Calling God "miracle-wreaking" presents a fascinating juxtaposition of terms. When Jesus cured the paralytic or multiplied the loaves and fishes, for example, was that an example of "miracle-wreaking"? If so, bring it on! As for the accusation of being "prayer-answering," I am hard-pressed to see what Dawkins finds so sinister here.

In forming their opinions about the biblical God, the atheists seem to be more fundamentalistic than the fundamentalists. They take every word of the sacred text at face value, with no attempt to sift through the evident anthropomorphisms to get a sense of who God is and what He is revealing about Himself. They ignore the literary genres at work and neglect to read the passages in context, which would give a more accurate idea of the God being presented. What they do, rather, is select a few texts where God comes off looking like the big bad wolf and paste them together as if they were the whole picture. What they fail to notice—willfully or not—is that the God revealed in the Old Testament is above all a just and faithful God, One who keeps His promises and forgives the many transgressions of His people.

I have searched in vain through these atheistic tracts for a balanced treatment of the biblical text. Where, for instance, are the numerous references to God's tenderness, His mercy, His love for His children, His patience, His desire for their well-being? Remember these consoling words from the Old Testament, where God asserts His faithfulness to His people:

Do not fear, for I have redeemed you;
I have called you by name, you are mine.
When you pass through the waters, I will be with you;

and through the rivers, they shall not overwhelm you;
when you walk through fire you shall not be burned,
and the flame shall not consume you.
For I am the LORD your God.

(Isaiah 43:1–3)

Or look further along look at the well-known passage where God's love is compared to that of a mother:

Can a woman forget her nursing child,
or show no compassion for the child of her womb?
Even these may forget,
yet I will not forget you.
See, I have inscribed you on the palms of my hands;
your walls are continually before me.

(Isaiah 49:14–16)

Elsewhere, God is often presented as a husband, full of love for His wife (His people). Despite the unfaithfulness of Israel, He keeps coming back, purifying her and taking her to Himself. He is not vindictive, but merciful. In the book of the prophet Hosea, we read the following description of God's love:

I will now allure her,
and bring her into the wilderness,

and speak tenderly to her.
From there I will give her her vineyards,
    and make the Valley of Achor a door of hope.
There she shall respond as in the days of her youth,
    as at the time when she came out of the land of
    Egypt.
On that day, says the LORD, you will call me,
    "My husband."

(Hosea 2:14–16)

Christians believe that God's self-revelation was progressive. The Bible didn't fall from heaven ready-made but was written over time. Israel's knowledge of God grew as well, as they contemplated His action in their history and meditated on His words. This self-revelation culminates in the person of Jesus Christ. As Paul wrote, "But when the fullness of time had come, God sent his Son, born of a woman, born under the law, in order to redeem those who were under the law, so that we might receive adoption" (Galatians 4:4–5). It is in Christ that the limitlessness of God's love for humanity is made fully clear.

The Bible presents God above all as a Father. This may be precisely what atheists find so disagreeable about Him. A father sometimes lays down the law. He exercises tough love. He makes demands. On reading the atheists' tirade against God, I couldn't help but think of a certain sort of adolescent outburst against one's father. Only fathers—it seems—merit such unmitigated fury.

In general, the atheists' portrayal of the biblical God is hopelessly unbalanced and tendentious. One would expect a little more from scientists and journalists—two professions that pride themselves on their impartiality. One thing for sure, the biblical God engenders very different reactions, from the deepest gratitude and devotion to the most passionate hatred. But maybe that says more about us than it does about God.

19.

Are the Gospels reliable historical documents?

ANOTHER CRITICISM VOICED BY NEARLY ALL atheists is the unreliability of the Bible—and specifically the four Gospels—as a historical document. Hitchens faults the Jewish scholar Maimonides for falling into "the same error as do the Christians, in assuming that the four gospels were in any sense a historical record" and adds for good measure that the Gospel authors "cannot agree on anything of importance" and the Gospels "are most certainly not literal truth."[1] This may seem strange, since elsewhere he uses this presumably unreliable source to postulate on whether Jesus ever thought He was God or intended to found a church, yet this is just one of the many paradoxes of these atheistic works.

Though none of these authors received formal training in theology or biblical exegesis, they allow themselves categorical assertions that would be unthinkable in other disciplines. In chapter 3 of *The God Delusion,* for example, Richard Dawkins puts on the hat of the biblicist and presumes to teach theologians about the Good Book. The outright errors in the section titled "Arguments from Scripture" are simply too many to enumerate here, but a few examples may prove illuminating.

Dawkins states: "Ever since the nineteenth century, scholarly theologians have made an overwhelming case that the gospels are not reliable accounts of what happened in the history of the real world."[2] One wonders how many theological works Dawkins read in order to make such a bold assertion. Never mind that he had already disqualified theology as a science; what he says here is simply false. While one can find biblical scholars to support virtually any conceivable interpretation of Scripture, there is nothing near unanimity in dismissing the historical value of the Gospel accounts. The Catholic position on this question, representing a mere 1.1 billion Christian believers, is stated succinctly in the 1965 dogmatic constitution on Divine Revelation, *Dei Verbum:* "[The] Church has firmly and with absolute constancy held, and continues to hold, that the four Gospels just named, whose historical character the Church unhesitatingly asserts, faithfully hand on what Jesus Christ, while living among men, really did and taught for their eternal salvation until the day He was taken up into heaven (see Acts 1:1)."[3]

Regarding the genesis of the canon of Sacred Scripture, Dawkins claims that the canonical Gospels "were chosen, more or less arbitrarily, out of a larger sample of at least a dozen including the Gospels of Thomas, Peter, Nicodemus, Philip, Bartholomew and Mary Magdalen."[4] Here it appears that he was taking theology classes from Dan Brown, since this summary of the formation of the New Testament looks as if it were lifted straight from *The Da Vinci Code*. He naively assumes that the mere title of "gospel" puts all the ancient texts on an equal footing, the same mistake made by Dan Brown and other purveyors of religious sensationalism. The fact is that the apocryphal "gospels" of Thomas, Philip, Mary, and others were rejected for serious reasons, such as the fact that they were written long after the accepted accounts, by non-eyewitnesses, to advance a dubious gnostic agenda.

Dawkins then states: "Nobody knows who the four evangelists were, but they almost certainly never met Jesus personally. Much of what they wrote was in no sense an honest attempt at history but was simply rehashed from the Old Testament, because the gospel-makers were devoutly convinced that the life of Jesus must fulfill Old Testament prophecies."[5] Where does he come up with this? On what authority can he state that the evangelists never knew Jesus? More incredible still, how can he judge the "honesty" of persons whose identity supposedly remains in the shadows of history?

Grave historical errors that can be begrudgingly swallowed in a work of *fiction* like Dan Brown's become downright unconscionable for someone claiming to be a rigorous scientist. If an author such as Dawkins were to work with such sloppy methodology in biology, he would quickly find himself booed out of the academy and looking for a job. I don't know what he would say if I—who have no more training in evolutionary biology than he does in theology—started pontificating on disputed questions of mammalogy, ornithology, or herpetology.

The fact remains that the four Gospels continue to this day to be the best historical documents we have relating to the life and deeds of Jesus Christ.

We have more than five thousand New Testament manuscripts, and many are dated within a few years of their authors' lives, which means that the historical documentary evidence for the New Testament far surpasses that of any other work of its time. Recent scholarship has shown moreover that the Gospels were penned much closer to the time of Jesus' death than previously thought, most certainly by eyewitnesses in the case of three out of four. Strong evidence points to a completion of the entire text of the New Testament before the year AD 100. The first three Gospels, for example, prophesied the fall of the temple of Jerusalem, which occurred in AD 70. However, the fulfillment of the prophecy is never mentioned, which suggests that it hadn't happened as of the writing of the text. There is a broad academic literature attesting to the historicity of the Gospels, such as Craig L. Blomberg's *The Historical Reliability of the Gospels* and F. F. Bruce's *The New Testament Documents: Are They Reliable?* to name just two.[6]

It is said that fools rush in where angels fear to tread. It appears that sometimes scientists and journalists make the same mistake.

20.

Did the historical Jesus really exist?

NOT CONTENT WITH KNOCKING SACRED TEXTS, our atheists cast doubt on the very existence of Jesus as a historical person. Dawkins, for instance, writes that it is possible "to mount a serious, though not widely supported, historical case that Jesus never lived at all."[1] For his part, Christopher Hitchens states that Jesus' existence is "highly questionable." What seems rather "highly questionable" is the rigor of Hitchens's fact-checking, since his work is strewn with factual errors. Three pages after announcing Jesus' nonexistence, he states that the Catholic doctrines of the Immaculate Conception and the Assumption of Mary were announced in the years 1852 and 1951 respectively, both of which are erroneous.[2] A simple Wikipedia search would have allowed him to ascertain the true dates of those pronouncements as December 8, 1854, and November 1, 1950. Never let it be said that atheists allow careful scholarship to get in the way of their antitheistic crusade!

The simple fact of the matter is that we "know" Jesus really existed insofar as we can know any historical fact. That is to say, none of us were present on the earth two thousand years ago to empirically verify Jesus' existence, so we must rely on the historical record. But the historical record is as conclusive as we could possibly hope for. As Theodore Dalrymple noted in *The City Journal*, "If I questioned whether George Washington died in 1799, I could spend a lifetime trying to prove it and find myself still, at the end of my efforts, having to make a leap, or perhaps several leaps, of faith in order to believe the rather banal fact that I had set out to prove."[3] In other words, what you believe depends on what you *are willing* to believe.

Plenty of scholars have undertaken to collect all ancient historical references to Jesus. It is not the case to repeat their findings here, except in very abridged form. The celebrated Roman historian Tacitus wrote of superstitious "Christians," who suffered under Pontius Pilate during the reign of Tiberius.[4] Suetonius, chief secretary to the emperor Hadrian, wrote that there was a man named Chrestus (or Christ) who lived during the first century.[5]

Julius Africanus quotes the historian Thallus in a discussion of the darkness that followed the crucifixion of Christ.[6] Pliny the Younger in his *Letters* recorded early Christian ritual practices such as their worship of Jesus as God and their celebration of the love feast and Lord's Supper, besides mentioning that these Christians were known to be very ethical.[7] Lucian of Samosata was a second-century Greek writer who stated that Jesus was worshipped by Christians, introduced new teachings, and was crucified for them. He wrote that Jesus' teachings included the brotherhood of believers, conversion, and the importance of denying other gods. Christians, wrote Lucian, lived according to Jesus' laws, believed themselves immortal, and were characterized by contempt for death, voluntary self-devotion, and renunciation of material goods.[8]

The Jewish historical record confirms Jesus' existence as well. The most famous ancient Jewish historian was Flavius Josephus, who, in his *Antiquities,* refers to James, "the brother of Jesus, who was called

Christ." There is a controversial verse (18:3) that says,

> At this time there was a wise man who was called Jesus. His conduct was good and (he) was known to be virtuous. And many people from among the Jews and the other nations became his disciples. Pilate condemned him to be crucified and to die. But those who had become his disciples did not abandon his discipleship. They reported that he had appeared to them three days after his crucifixion, and that he was alive; accordingly he was perhaps the Messiah, concerning whom the prophets have recounted wonders.[9]

The Babylonian Talmud confirms Jesus' crucifixion on the eve of Passover, and the accusations against Christ of practicing sorcery and encouraging Jewish apostasy.[10]

All of these writers, without exception, lived in or close to the time of Jesus. None were Christian or had anything evident to gain from reporting about Jesus. The rapid spread of Christianity after Jesus' death and resurrection is amazing enough, in that it evidences the credibility (in Jesus' case) of the incredible claim that a human being—one known to the believers—is God Himself. But it is difficult indeed to imagine that Jesus' disciples, a handful of fisher-men, succeeded in deluding so many serious writers of their own time about the very existence of their Messiah!

Most important, however, the texts of the New Testament itself provide the best historical informa-tion we have about Jesus' life and teachings. Their unabashed historical assertions about Jesus were written not many years after His death, when many contemporaries of Jesus were still alive. The fact that there is no record of any contemporary refut-ing these claims, or asserting that Jesus never lived, is ample historical evidence that He did indeed live. To deny this is to reject the clear historical record in favor of a personal agenda.

Still, perhaps the clearest evidence of Jesus' his-torical existence is the witness of literally thousands of Christians in the first century AD, including the twelve apostles, who were willing to give their lives as martyrs for Jesus Christ. They could have escaped death by disowning Christ or stepping forward to say that it all had been a hoax. This didn't happen. Some people will die for what they believe to be true; no one will die for what they know to be a lie.

21.

> Did Jesus found the church, or was
> He co-opted by His followers?

ATHEISTS MAY RAIL AGAINST GOD, BUT THEY reserve a special disdain for organized religion. Thus, though they may question whether Jesus ever existed and argue that the Gospels tell us nothing about Him, they are more than ready to assert categorically that He never intended to found a church. How they could know this without the help of the Gospel record is a true miracle of atheist logic. Hitchens, for example, states that Jesus' disciples "had no idea that anyone would ever found a church on their master's announcements" and that Jesus Himself evidenced "complete indifference to the founding of any temporal church."[1]

This is a tough claim to process. The idea of church was a familiar concept to early Christians, who universally understood it to be founded by Jesus Christ. The New Testament is replete with references to the church. Writing in the first century, the apostle Paul refers to the "church" (*ekklesia*) some five dozen times in his letters, and there is no record of anyone standing up and accusing him of innovating something that Jesus never intended. He speaks variously of the visible church as Christ's body, as Christ's spotless bride, as the community of Christian believers, as the household of God, as the pillar and bulwark of the truth. He moreover writes of "deacons," "presbyters," and "bishops"—giving good evidence that a differentiated Christian clergy was in existence as of the first century.

The apostle John uses the term "church" several times in his third epistle, and another twenty-odd times in the book of Revelation, whose authorship is generally attributed to him. The apostle Peter uses the term "church" in his first letter, and it can be found in the Letter of James as well. All three of these men formed part of the original band of twelve apostles, who, according to Christopher Hitchens, "had no idea that anyone would ever found a church." Either they quickly gathered in a conspiracy to undermine their Lord's wishes, for which there is no historical evidence, or Hitchens has got the story dead wrong.

But let us turn to the witness of Jesus Himself. Hitchens doesn't even acknowledge the text that most clearly contradicts his claim. Matthew's Gospel records Jesus saying to Peter, in front of the other disciples, "I tell you, you are Peter, and on this rock I will build my church, and the gates of Hades will not prevail against it" (Matthew 16:18). Unlike other thinkers and founders, Jesus left nothing in writing; what we do find is a stated intention to establish a church.

What other evidence can be found of Jesus' project? He carefully selected twelve "apostles" and set them apart from His many followers. He gave them special training as well as explaining many things to them in private that He didn't announce to more general gatherings. This number twelve mirrored the twelve tribes of Israel, the "people of God," and expresses an intention to establish a new Israel.

Early Christians attributed significance to this special "college" of apostles surrounding Jesus. When Judas, one of the twelve, betrayed Jesus and later committed suicide, the Christian community hastened to appoint someone else to take his place (Acts 1:15–26).

The appointment of successors to the apostles underscores the Christians' sense that the apostles represented an institutional structure that was meant to continue through time, rather than a mere group of individuals. The apostles left behind them a structured community, under the guidance of acknowledged pastors, who built and sustained it. This was understood by all to be a fulfillment of the express wishes of Jesus.

The atheistic authors' attempts at biblical exegesis fall flat, and the best advice they could receive is not to give up their day jobs. Jesus not only intended to found a church—He really did so.

22.

Do Christians hate sex? Does faith
encourage sexual repression?

ATHEISTIC CRITICISMS OF CHRISTIANITY ARE NOT
limited to the authority of the Bible or the
institution of the church. Key elements of Christian
teaching also come under fire, and first among these
is sexual morality. Christopher Hitchens remarks
that "Christianity is too repressed to offer sex in paradise" and repeats the old canard that religion—and
God—are antisex, leading to "holy dread of the pro-
creative act and its associated impulses and necessi-
ties." Religious faith is "both the result and the cause
of dangerous sexual repression," says Hitchens[1] (as
if sexual repression were one of the twenty-first
century's most serious problems!). Yet nonbelievers

easily forget that, according to the biblical account, the first commandment God issued to man and woman was "Be fruitful and multiply" (Genesis 1:28). To put it quite frankly, God's first edict to His new creation looked a lot like "Have sex!"

Since Hitchens begins with his conclusions, no religion can get sex right. Therefore, Hitchens complains on the one hand that Jesus had *too few* offspring, while Muhammad had *too many*. Like Goldilocks in the famous bedtime story, for whom one bed was too hard and another too soft, for Hitchens sex has to be "just right," which is the same as saying it must follow Hitchens's own proclivities. These proclivities are not hard to plumb, as he asserts with the gravest authority: "Clearly, the human species is designed to experiment with sex."[2]

Making Christians out to be sex-haters is just a corollary of the bigger myth that Jesus was history's greatest party pooper; in a world where the party must be an orgy, sexual restraint becomes the worst expression of this ill humor. Yet anyone who takes the time to see what Jesus and Christians after Him *really* think about sex finds that the opposite is true. Jesus is, after all, the one whose stated purpose was "that they might have life, and have it in abundance" (John 10:10). Jesus didn't come to put a damper on human joy, but to bring it to fulfillment. It's true that Christianity doesn't encourage rampant sexual incontinence, but the aim is not to lessen joy but to increase it. A measure of self-restraint leads to greater happiness than reckless abandon.

Granted, Christianity has not been immune to the temptation of Manichaeanism with its disdain for matter and the body, and a puritanical spirit has occasionally made inroads into Christian thought, but it is Christians themselves who have always chased it out again. More recent Christian theology has been especially noteworthy in this regard. Some have made the case that the most important contribution of Pope John Paul II to Christian thought was his remarkable five-year catechetical series dubbed *Man and Woman He Created Them: A Theology of the Body*.[3] In these discourses John Paul showed the beauty of human sexuality as a particularly eloquent reflection of God's own love.

Even the ancient Christian tradition of celibacy (see Matthew 19:12; 1 Corinthians 7:7–19) does not reflect a disdain for sexuality, but the greatest appreciation for it. People do not sacrifice worthless things to God, but only the very best things. Moreover, celibacy has never been promoted as a vocation for the majority, but rather for the few who are called to imitate the Lord more closely, to dedicate themselves totally to the service of the church, and to bear witness to the primacy of the things of heaven over the things of the earth. The presence of committed celibate men and women in our midst reminds us of the power of God's love to fill the human heart, and that the world as we know it "is passing away" (1 Corinthians 7:31).

It was not a Christian, however, but a twenty-three-year-old orthodox Jew by the name of Wendy Shalit who in 1999 penned the eye-opening book *A Return to Modesty: Discovering the Lost Virtue.* In it, Ms. Shalit made an impressive case for the value of modesty—get this—for *sustaining* sexual interest and keeping people from becoming jaded and uninterested in sex. It is not repression but overindulgence in sex, she argues persuasively, that robs it of its beauty, fascination, and pleasure. When sex is cheapened, commercialized, and stripped of sacredness, the result is not titillation but boredom.[4]

Shalit's findings seem to find an echo in studies done correlating religious practice with sexual satisfaction. The 1994 Sex in America survey found that very religious women enjoy a higher level of sexual satisfaction in their marriages than nonreligious women. Similarly, various independent studies have concluded that men with no religious affiliation consistently report a lower level of marital satisfaction than those of any religion whatsoever.[5]

In their 2003 book *The Psychology of Religion: An Empirical Approach,* researcher Bernard Spilka and his colleagues found that religion had, if anything, a positive influence on sexual satisfaction. In their 1970 work *Human Sexual Inadequacy,* sexologists William Masters and Virginia Johnson suggested that religion probably caused adverse effects on sexual pleasure. Yet contrary to the untested indictments of Masters and Johnson, Spilka and his team found the opposite to be true. Reported sexual activity levels are actually *higher* for very religious respondents than for those who are not religious. Spilka sums up his findings with the statement "Religion appears to be no barrier or impediment to sexually gratifying relations."[6] So much for religion stifling sex.

Hitchens's attacks on religion often thinly veil his own prejudices and penchants. Such, for example, is his diagnosis of sexual prohibitions as a result of repressed desire. Hitchens breezily affirms: "Nothing optional—from homosexuality to adultery—is ever made punishable unless those who do the prohibiting...have a repressed desire to participate."[7] That is quite a statement. So anything we find reprehensible reflects an innate, hidden wish to do the same? Our censure of rape, for instance, would evidence a repressed desire to be rapists? Or our reproach of torture, would that conceal an uncon-fessable urge to engage in similar practices? Or does this psychological principle apply only to sex? I understand that Hitchens is a journalist and cannot be expected to possess expertise in every field. With all due respect, however, one would think that he could refrain from repeating accusations that fly in the face of the facts.

PART V

ATHEISM UNDER THE MICROSCOPE

Enough for defense. In this final section we will turn the tables on atheists for a moment to see what atheism has to offer on its own merits. If, as many atheistic authors insist, atheism furnishes a better alternative to religious belief, its benefits should be evident. What are the real fruits of atheism for both the individual and society?

Our first order of business deals with the modern "virtue" of tolerance. Since atheists accuse religious people of intolerance, it is only fair to ask whether atheism offers something better. Are atheists characterized by tolerance in their dealings with people who disagree with them? Are their proposals for society marked by a greater respect for the beliefs of all, or rather by a more restrictive worldview whereby everyone is required to march in lockstep with their new orthodoxy?

The second question deals with citizenship. The atheists suggest that the exclusion of God from one's outlook on life makes a person a more responsible citizen. Is this true? What exactly does atheism add to a person's commitment to the common good? And if atheism is a positive good for society, why did philosophers like John Locke suggest that atheists should be excluded from public life?

Next we will look at the moral framework of atheism. Having unconvincingly criticized Christian morality, what does atheism offer in its place? Do atheists make a cogent proposal for a more humane moral code, or do they rather undermine the very foundations of morality? Does evolutionism perhaps provide a more convincing ethical standard than traditional Judeo-Christian principles?

Our final two chapters will address the question of atheism's fruitfulness on a personal level. What effects does atheistic "belief" produce in its adherents? Does atheism make people happy? Do those who reject God describe themselves as generally satisfied with life and hopeful about the future, or are they rather less happy than believers?

On a related note, does atheism make individuals more generous with their fellow men and women? If, as these authors claim, the atheist ethic is superior to the Christian moral code, what are the tangible results of this moral awakening? Do atheists donate more money to humanitarian causes than their religious counterparts? Are atheists more generous in volunteering their time and skills to the community?

As alert readers may already guess, atheists don't score well on these questions. Read on to see how the atheist proposal looks more and more dismal the further one moves beyond their rhetoric to look at the facts.

23.

Are atheists more tolerant
than believers?

A THEISTS COMPLAIN OF THE INTOLERANCE OF religious folk, which usually boils down to believers' enthusiasm in announcing the tenets of their faith to the world. Thus, as we have seen, Christopher Hitchens complains that all he wants is that religious people *"leave me alone,"*[1] whereas Sam Harris complains of the nasty letters he received after writing *The End of Faith,* urging him to mend his ways, abandon his atheism, and believe in the good news before it's too late. Harris says that many who claim to be transformed by Christ's love "are deeply, even murderously, intolerant of criticism."[2]

Despite this hyperbole, all in all, religious intolerance, at least in present-day America, seems rather
innocuous. I know of no Christians who believe
that atheism or rival creeds should be illegal. I see
no movements afoot to pillory atheists or segre-
gate Methodists. Religious liberty and freedom of
conscience are the hard-won spoils of Western civilization. Christians hold that faith and worship must
be freely given to be of any value at all and soundly
reject the idea that religious belief can be compulsory. Though some fanatics may disagree, all the
major religions now subscribe to the premise that
religion must not be advanced by the sword.

How do our atheistic friends measure up on the
tolerance scale? Not very well, it turns out. Sometimes
the intolerance of atheists takes the form of simple
verbal abuse. Christopher Hitchens writes that religion is "violent, irrational, intolerant, allied to racism and tribalism and bigotry" and "comes from the
bawling and fearful infancy of our species, and is a
babyish attempt to meet our inescapable demand for
knowledge." Similarly, religious people are worthy of
nothing but contempt. Hitchens calls Augustine "a
self-centered fantasist and an earth-centered ignora-
mus," while Billy Graham is a mere exploiter "whose
record of opportunism and anti-Semitism is in itself a

minor national disgrace." Moses was "fanatical," John Calvin "a sadist," and Mahatma Gandhi an "obscurantist" who imposed "his ego." John the Evangelist's book of Revelation consists of "deranged fantasies," while the apostle Paul harbors "both fear and contempt for the female." All it takes to gain Hitchens's undying scorn is to espouse religious faith.[3]

Yet at other times atheistic intolerance goes beyond mere name-calling. In *The End of Faith,* Sam Harris ominously announces: "Words like 'God' and 'Allah' must go the way of 'Apollo' and 'Baal,' or they will unmake our world." Whereas earlier he had excoriated Christians for their supposed intolerance, suddenly he does an about-face and starts inciting his co-irreligionists to active *intolerance* of religion. He makes the frightening claim that the ideal of religious tolerance "is one of the principal forces driving us toward the abyss." "Given the link between belief and action," he adds, "we can no more tolerate a diversity of religious beliefs than a diversity of beliefs about epidemiology and basic hygiene."[4] Yes, you read correctly. *Religious tolerance* is the culprit, and must be done away with. No longer should people be allowed to believe whatever they choose. They must abandon faith or pay the consequences.

And what are these consequences? Harris doesn't

leave us guessing. "The link between belief and behavior raises the stakes considerably. Some propositions are so dangerous that it may be ethical to kill people for believing them. This may seem an extraordinary claim, but it merely enunciates an ordinary fact about the world in which we live."[5] Taken aback, reviewer Theodore Dalrymple wrote that these words were "quite possibly the most disgraceful that I have read in a book by a man posing as a rationalist."[6]

This atheistic intolerance is not aimed only at religious fanatics. Remember, for Harris, Hitchens, and Dawkins, religious extremism is not the main problem. Moderate religion is even more worrisome, because it anesthetizes us to the dangers inherent in religion itself. Thus Harris writes that "the greatest problem confronting civilization is not merely religious extremism: rather, it is the larger set of cultural and intellectual accommodations we have made to faith itself. Religious moderates are, in large part, responsible for the religious conflict in our world."[7] No more Mr. Nice Guy. No more treating religious believers as worthy of respect. Religion must die.

Harris isn't alone in the extremism of his antireligious views. Though Hitchens claims that he would not prohibit religious faith even if he thought he could, he still quotes Karl Marx at length with evident admiration, where the latter expresses his view that "the *abolition of religion* as the illusory happiness of the people is required for their real happiness" (emphasis added).[8] Not even a generation has passed since the fall of the Berlin Wall, and Hitchens seems already to have forgotten the catastrophe of humanity's attempts to eradicate religion and impose atheism on the people. Does Hitchens really contend that real Marxism, in any of its incarnations, ushered in the earthly paradise envisioned by its founder?

On reading these atheistic tracts, one walks away with the uncomfortable feeling that, if given half the chance, at least some of the authors would embrace laws banning religious practice. Despite their protestations, it seems that Hitchens, Dawkins, and others of the atheists' guild are the ones prepared to roll back freedom of conscience to make all citizens walk together in atheistic lockstep. Where is the outrage from reasonable people? Is atheistic intolerance—the most devastating form of intolerance in history—the one form that gets a pass?

24.

Are atheists better citizens than religious folk?

CHRISTOPHER HITCHENS AND RICHARD DAWKINS frequently quote their favorite Enlightenment figures, especially the American Thomas Jefferson, to back up their position. One important figure these authors refrain from mentioning is a hero of Jefferson's: the British Enlightenment philosopher John Locke. In his celebrated *Letter Concerning Toleration*, Locke asks whether all sorts of religious belief should be tolerated in society. Almost all, he answers. Conspicuous among those whom Locke thought should *not* be tolerated were the atheists. Locke wrote that:

> Those are not at all to be tolerated who deny the Being of a God.... Promises, Covenants, and Oaths, which

are the Bonds of Humane Society, can have no hold upon an Atheist. The taking away of God, tho but even in Thought, dissolves all.... Besides also, those that by their Atheism undermine and destroy all Religion, can have no Pretence of Religion whereupon to challenge the Privilege of a Toleration.[1]

Locke's words are interesting, not because atheists should not be tolerated, but because of the reasons he gives for his opinion. Locke thought that the elimination of God (even in thought) removed eternal accountability for one's actions, and that those who lacked such accountability were not to be trusted. I have no doubt that there are many responsible, honest atheists. At the same time, I am left with the lingering suspicion that Locke may have been onto something. We human beings can be so weak, so fickle, and so downright petty at times that most of us need as much incentive as possible to do the right thing, especially when it is difficult. The conviction that we will one day meet our Maker and be required to render an accounting for our actions can often be the weight that tips the scales. Even aside from the taking of oaths, who would want to be governed by someone who scoffs at the idea of final justice, rewards and punishments, human dignity, and accountability to a Being infinitely greater than ourselves?

Without a Supreme Being or a universal recognition of truth, atheists, agnostics, and humanists alike have some very big problems on their hands if they are to establish a successful or even functional worldview. Without God or some type of moral base, there is an enormous missing component that is essential for establishing a societal framework. Atheism doesn't usually become popular on its own steam but does so by standing on the shoulders of healthy social and moral frameworks provided by the great religions of the world. In the name of intellectual enlightenment, godlessness provides members of usually affluent societies a temporary escape from day-to-day rules of life and good behavior, as defined by their host religion.

In the end, however, the only alternative to moral truth is force. Where a unified concept of right and wrong has been abandoned and moral accountability flushed away, all we have left is competing subjective worldviews. The strongest will triumph, and a tyrannical oligarchy—a new "moral" (or immoral) majority—will end up forcing its political correctness on everyone else.

Once again, a cost-benefit analysis of this sort does nothing to prove or disprove the existence of God or the truth of this or that religion. What it does do, quite satisfactorily to my mind, is dispel the myth that atheists are somehow better citizens than their religious counterparts. The absence of God adds nothing to one's civic character, and more often than not detracts from it. The removal of God leaves Caesar unchallenged and easily paves the way for totalitarianism. Historically, the ability of religious people to appeal to a higher moral authority than that of the state has been an effective force in keeping the state in check.

Christopher Hitchens's brother Peter, who is a Christian, tells us Christopher likes to tease that a world ruled by faith is like North Korea, a country where all is known and all is ordered. He has it backward. As Peter notes, North Korea is the opposite of a land ruled by truth and conscience. It is a land ruled by "men who do not believe in God or conscience, where nobody can be trusted to make his own choices, and where the State decides for the people what is right and what is wrong. And it is the ultimate destination of atheistic thought."[2]

25.

Are atheists more ethical than
religious believers?

SINCE ATHEISTS HAVE GONE TO GREAT LENGTHS TO
show that much evil has been done in the name
of religion, it is only fair to ask how atheists stand up
to believers in the area of morality. I won't bother to
document the volumes of blood shed in the twenti-
eth century in the name of atheism, but I will look
more deeply at why atheism cannot provide a working ethical system.

I've mentioned that Hitchens refers to four "irreducible objections" to religious faith. Here I would
like to introduce my own four "irreducible objections" to an atheistic morality. First, a purely materialistic ethic attributes no inherent worth to a human

being, so what is done to a person has no real moral value. Second, right and wrong lose all meaning as categories in a merely material world. Third, a true materialist must deny free will, and thus moral accountability. Fourth, an evolutionary ethic is necessarily bloodthirsty and cruel.

First, as regards the value of the human person, I would appeal to my readers' common sense. Which theory regarding human beings would more likely produce a humane ethic: one that considers man to possess singular worth in the eyes of his Creator, or one that believes man to be a hunk of matter with no greater intrinsic value than a manure heap? What rational justification can there be to treat one lump of matter any differently from another, except perhaps the possible repercussions for oneself? If there is no God, and everything is reduced to chemical reactions, who is to say that the ethical opinion voiced by your particular blob of matter is any better than Saddam Hussein's?

Hitchens, in fact, faults Christianity for attributing far *too much* value to human beings. He writes that religion teaches people to be self-centered by assuring them "that god cares for them individually," whereas in reality, "our place in the cosmos is so unimaginably small that we cannot, with our miserable endowment of cranial matter, contemplate it for long at all. No less difficult is the realization that we may also be quite random as presences on earth."[1]

Yet once we eliminate man's special standing in the universe, our morality falls apart as well. The only reason for treating a fellow human being with any respect is left to our volatile inclination to do so versus the negative consequences of not doing so. Where these moral sanctions are absent, there is no rational reason to treat a human being any better than a stone. Throughout his work, Hitchens repeatedly refers to human beings simply as "mammals" to reiterate that we are just one species among many, but this leads one to the uncomfortable conclusion that for Hitchens, there is no real moral difference between a man and a field mouse.

Second, "right" and "wrong" ultimately mean nothing to a materialist. Actions may be practical or impractical, pleasant or painful, useful or useless, but they can never be "noble," "virtuous," or "good." The words *good* and *bad, better* and *worse,* are empirically meaningless, as are expressions such as "human dignity," "rights," or "duties." There may be an instinctual reaction to witnessing others' pain that inspires a sort of compassion, but there can be no rational defense of justice or moral behavior of any kind, short of the Hobbesian self-interested pacts that pre-serve our own hides. The scary thing is that atheists have nowhere to go for moral guidance, other than to their own feelings. For a true materialist, there are no grounds for value judgments.

Think about the consequences of that position. The Holocaust cannot be judged to be morally wrong. The terrorist acts of 9/11 cannot be judged to be morally wrong. The Columbine High School and Virginia Tech massacres cannot be judged to be morally wrong. The true materialist can coher-ently say and do nothing regarding right and wrong. And what's more, a materialistic nonethic inevitably results in the types of moral disasters I've just men-tioned. Ideas do have consequences, and atheists would do well to recall that as they wield their pens in an attempt to forge an atheistic society.

Christopher Hitchens's brother Peter reviewed *God Is Not Great.* Peter offered the following devastat-ing analysis of the ethical pretensions Christopher put forward:

He even refers to "conscience" and makes frequent thunderous denunciations of various evil actions. Where is his certain knowledge of what is right and wrong supposed to have come from? How can the idea of a conscience have any meaning in a world of random chance, where in the end we are all just collections of molecules swirling in a purposeless confusion? If you are getting inner promptings, why should you pay any attention to them? It is as absurd as the idea of a compass with no magnetic North. You might as well take moral instruction from your bile duct.[2]

Third, true materialists end up denying free will and human accountability. In this regard Richard Dawkins is surprisingly (but self-destructively) consistent with his materialism. He makes no bones about denying free will, but in so doing, he wipes out ethics as well:

> As scientists, we believe that human brains, though they may not work in the same way as man-made computers, are as surely governed by the laws of physics. When a computer malfunctions, we do not punish it. We track down the problem and fix it, usually by replacing a damaged component, either in hardware or software.
>
> Isn't the murderer or the rapist just a machine with a defective component? Or a defective upbringing? Defective education? Defective genes?
>
> But doesn't a truly scientific, mechanistic view of

the nervous system make nonsense of the very idea of responsibility? Any crime, however heinous, is in principle to be blamed on antecedent conditions acting through the accused's physiology, heredity and environment.[3]

This denial of free will leads to the necessary conclusion that you can simply shrug off personal responsibility for all of your choices (apparent choices, since we are no more free than a chrysanthemum or a food processor). Maybe the devil didn't make you do it, but surely your genes and environment did. Christians do not deny the influence of genes and culture on human behavior but still affirm basic human freedom. Whereas genes may lead a horse to bad water, they cannot make him drink it.

Imagine if we tried to apply Dawkins's reasoning in our real lives. Gone are the ideas of virtue and vice. Gone are praise and blame. Our "choices" are reduced to chemical reactions and secretions within the body. "It's not that you're good, Johnny, it's just that your glands are really secreting well these days..." How absurdly unscientific! Dawkins begins his paragraph with the statement "As scientists, we believe..." Weren't the hard sciences all about hypothesis and verification? Wasn't Dawkins opposed to "belief"? It seems only *scientific* belief gets a hearing.

Fourth, if atheists reject traditional ethics, what do they offer in exchange? The only model left to them is that offered by evolution: the survival of the fittest. Yet does evolution provide a moral model that is more humane than that offered by the Christian God? Though Christopher Hitchens contends that the "Golden Rule" is fruit of the evolution of the species, he admits that evolution is "callous and cruel, and also capricious."[4] For his part, Richard Dawkins writes: "The logic of Darwinism concludes that the unit in the hierarchy of life which survives and passes through the filter of natural selection will tend to be selfish. The units that survive in the world will be the ones that succeeded in surviving at the expense of their rivals at their own level in the hierarchy."[5]

Dawkins describes a couple of rare examples where altruism seems to benefit individuals of the species, but these are clearly an attempt to justify a theory rather than draw the logical conclusions from the facts. An evolutionary ethic takes as its core concept the struggle for survival, the victory of the fittest, and successful adaptation. Survival of the fittest—translated into ethics—always means that the biggest, strongest, and wiliest get the food and the mates.

Is this the sort of ethical model that our society needs in order to become more caring, more just, more welcoming, and more authentically human? Even when people try to dress it up in a more attractive guise, it remains a bloodthirsty ethic. Here the attempt to distill rationality out of what is in itself irrational necessarily fails.

These four irreducible objections to a materialistic ethic show the bankruptcy of a worldview that refuses to recognize spiritual realities. Atheists may well reach the conclusion of Friedrich Nietzsche that human life is absurd, and that there is no value to life or our actions other than the value we impose upon them. This is the nihilism that logically and necessarily flows from materialism. In Nietzsche's case, it also led to Nazism.

Above all, let not atheists attempt to take the moral high ground of possessing a "higher ethic." The very expression is meaningless to a materialistic worldview, where all moral choices are ultimately the result of random happenstance.

26.

Are atheists happier than believers?

I N *GOD IS NOT GREAT,* CHRISTOPHER HITCHENS asks why belief does not make its adherents happy.[1] If biblical claims are true, he wonders, why aren't believers happier than atheists? Yet is this the case? Are believers really less happy than nonbelievers?

We could fall back on more anecdotal evidence, of the sort indulged in by our authors. "All my atheistic friends are really happy folks," or "Let me tell you about a religious person I met who was really sad," or "I think I would be sadder if I were religious..." Fortunately, however, we don't need to rely on this sort of flimsy argumentation, since numerous surveys have already been conducted, anonymously asking people about their faith and life satisfaction. Here the data tell a very different story from that presented by atheists.[2]

Let's look first at the United States, one of the most believing nations in the world and (coincidentally?) the most prosperous. When it comes to religious practice, Americans can be divided into three categories. According to surveys, about 30 percent attend religious services at least once per week (we could call this group "religious"), while about 20 percent never attend (we could call this group "secular"). The rest attend sometimes, but irregularly. Despite other societal changes, these percentages have changed relatively little in past decades.[3]

So, how do religious Americans stand up to secular Americans when it comes to happiness? In 2004, the General Social Survey asked a sample of Americans, "Would you say that you are very happy, pretty happy, or not too happy?" Religious people were more than twice as likely as the secular to say they were "very happy" (43 percent versus 21 percent). Meanwhile, secular people were nearly *three times* as likely as the religious to say they were "not too happy" (21 percent versus 8 percent). In the same survey, religious people were more than a third more likely than the secular to say they were optimistic about the future (34 percent versus 24 percent).[4]

The happiness divide between religious and secular people does not stem from race, gender, or financial factors. Consider two people who are identical in every important way—income, education, age, sex, family status, race, and political views. The only difference is that the first person is religious and the second is secular. The religious person will still be *twice as likely* as the secular person to say that he or she is very happy.

What happens when we move outside of the United States? It turns out that the correlation between religiosity and personal satisfaction doesn't seem to depend on nationality at all, since researchers have found similar results in other countries. Nor does it depend on denomination or religious creed. The 2000 Social Capital Community Benchmark Survey shows that practicing Protestants, Catholics, Jews, Muslims, and people from other religions are all far more likely than secularists to say they are happy. The happiness divide still holds up when we measure religiosity by some standard other than the frequency with which people attend religious services. For example, people who pray every day are a third more likely to be "very happy" than those who never pray, whether or not they attend services.[5]

What about the folks in the middle, who identify

with a faith but practice inconsistently? They are generally happier than secular people, but not as happy as regular practitioners. There is an interesting twist here, however, when it comes to the fear of death. One recent study found that as people get older, religious and secular people are less afraid of the grave than those in the middle, suggesting a relationship between fear of death and a religious practice inconsistent with one's faith.[6]

Obviously, not all religious people are happy and not all atheists are sad. Moreover, the happiness gauge says nothing about the *truth* of religion. Just because religion tends to make people happier doesn't mean that it's right. These statistics do put to rest, however, the specious claims of atheists who assert that religion makes people *less* happy. The exact opposite is true. Once again, when held up to the light, the case for atheism looks not only false, but downright fraudulent.

27.

Are atheists more generous and philanthropic than their religious counterparts?

W HEN SPEAKING ABOUT THE INFLUENCE OF religion on people, atheists are careful to tiptoe around the issue of charitable activity. The closest Christopher Hitchens comes is a rather vague and subjective assertion that no statistic will ever find that atheists "commit more crimes of greed or violence than the faithful."[1] The reason that atheists studiously avoid the question of generosity is that the results show an overwhelming difference between believers and nonbelievers. Not surprisingly, the difference favors believers.

In the year 2000, researchers at U.S. universities and the Roper Center for Public Opinion Research undertook the massive Social Capital Community Benchmark Survey (SCCBS), drawing thirty thousand observations from fifty communities across the United States. The survey questioned individuals about their "civic behavior," including their giving and volunteering during the year preceding the survey.[2]

Analyzing the data, Professor Arthur C. Brooks of Syracuse University divided respondents into three groups. He referred to the respondents who reported attending religious services every week or more often as "religious." This group made up 33 percent of the sample. Brooks called those who reported attending religious services less than a few times per year or explicitly saying they had no religion as "secular." These people made up 26 percent of the sample, leaving those who practiced their religion occasionally to make up the remaining 41 percent.[3]

Brooks found the variance between "religious" and "secular" giving to be dramatic. Religious people are 25 percentage points more likely than secularists to donate money (91 percent versus 66 percent) and 23 points more likely to volunteer time (67 percent versus 44 percent). In real dollars this translates into an average annual giving of $2,210 per person among the religious as compared to $642 among the secular. Regarding hours volunteered, religious people were found to volunteer an average of 12 times per year, while secular people volunteer an average of 5.8 times. To put this into perspective, religious people make up 33 percent of the population but are responsible for 52 percent of donations and account for 45 percent of times volunteered. Secular people make up 26 percent of the population but contribute 13 percent of the dollars and 17 percent of the times volunteered.[4]

Interestingly, these data show that the determining factor in predicting charitable behavior is not so much one's particular religion, but rather the seriousness of one's religious commitment. For example, among those who attend worship services regularly, 92 percent of Protestants give charitably, compared with 91 percent of Catholics, 91 percent of Jews, and 89 percent from other religions.[5]

Another indicative finding of the SCCBS study relates to giving to nonreligious charities. It turns out that religious people are more generous than secular people with nonreligious as well as religious causes. While 68 percent of the total population gives (and 51 percent volunteers) to nonreligious causes each year, religious people are 10 points more likely to give to these causes than secularists (71 percent versus 61 percent) and 21 points more likely to volunteer (60 percent versus 39 percent). As examples, religious people are 7 points more likely than secularists to volunteer for neighborhood and civic groups, 20 points more likely to volunteer to help the poor or elderly, and 26 points more likely to volunteer for school or youth programs. Across the board, religious practice is directly correlated to generosity with both time and money.[6]

These results are surprising only to someone with an ingrained antireligious prejudice. Even the deist Voltaire, no friend to Christianity, was forced to admit the great benefit of religion to organized charity: "Perhaps there is nothing greater on earth than the sacrifices of youth and beauty, often of high birth, made by the gentle sex in order to work in hospitals for the relief of human misery, the sight of which is so revolting to our delicacy. Peoples separated from the Roman religion have imitated but imperfectly so generous a charity."[7]

In his analysis of charitable giving and faith, Professor Brooks ends with a look at religion's pedagogical influence over giving and volunteering:

> Houses of worship might teach their congregants the religious duty to give, and about both the physical and spiritual needs of the poor. Simply put, people may

be more likely to learn charity inside a church, synagogue, or mosque than outside. If charity is indeed a learned behavior, it may be that houses of worship are only one means (albeit an especially efficacious one) to teach it.[8]

Atheistic writings rely almost exclusively on anecdotal evidence to make their case against religion. In asserting the superiority of atheism over religious belief, they simply string together vignettes showing everything bad they can think of done in the name of religion, in the hope that their horrible stories will disgust readers enough to turn them away from religion. Yet wherever a real comparison can be made between religious people and unbelievers, the statistical evidence always favors believers. Whether we speak about the evils and bloodshed of atheistic regimes, the generosity and charitable giving of religious people, or simply the happiness derived from religious faith, religion beats atheism hands-down in every area. This fact alone will give pause to any unbiased observer.

Epilogue: An Appeal to Christians

I WOULD LIKE TO CLOSE THIS SHORT BOOK WITH A personal appeal to my brothers and sisters in Christ. As evidently unfair and frustrating the attacks of the likes of Hitchens, Dawkins, Harris, and Dennett are, we can draw an important lesson from them.

We rightly complain that the enemies of Christianity rail against stereotypes of Christianity rather than the real thing, and that they choose the most egregious examples of Christians behaving in an unchristian way in order to cast aspersion on Christ and His church. Yet these authors also call us to an examination of conscience. We are, as the great

Saint Paul reminds us, "ambassadors for Christ" (2 Corinthians 5:20), challenged "to lead a life worthy of the calling to which you have been called" (Ephesians 4:1). When we fail to do so, we render ourselves accountable for the errors of others.

Jesus called His disciples to be salt of the earth and a light to the world. Importantly, He enjoined His followers: "Let your light shine before others, so that they may see your good works and give glory to your Father in heaven" (Matthew 5:16). These "good works" of Christians testify to God's truthfulness and inspire all to give Him glory.

Paul exhorts us: "Let your gentleness be known to everyone" (Philippians 4:5) and "Let your speech always be gracious" (Colossians 4:6). Yet how many, who now call themselves atheists or agnostics, were turned off by a self-righteous or impatient Christian who misrepresented the goodness and mercy of God? How many have never known Christ, because those called to preach Him to the world failed to do so with the spirit of service meant to characterize the followers of Jesus? How many times has the beauty of the Good News of Jesus Christ been distorted by the sins of His disciples?

True, we are all sinners. Thankfully, the message of salvation does not depend on us, and none of us will ever fully live up to our ideal. Still, I am convinced that the strongest argument for the truth of Christianity will come not from the pen of a theologian, but from the lives of saintly Christians filled with the Holy Spirit, who bear witness to God's passionate love for the world.

For some, no number of good examples will suffice. For some, especially those who have definitely renounced God's love, only a special grace of God will be able to open their closed hearts. Yet for many others the example of Christ's love incarnated in His followers is all that is necessary for them to turn to Him for salvation. When they see "your good works" they will feel compelled to "give glory to your Father in heaven."

I began this brief discourse recalling the words of the apostle Peter, who urged Christians: "Always be ready to make your defense to anyone who demands from you an accounting for the hope that is in you; yet do it with gentleness and reverence" (1 Peter 3:15–16). May his words enlighten all of us, that we may be worthy ambassadors of so great a King.

Notes

PART I: RELIGION IN THE CROSSHAIRS

1. Christopher Hitchens, *God Is Not Great: How Religion Poisons Everything* (New York: Twelve, 2007), 52.

CHAPTER 1: RELIGION OR RELIGIONS?
ARE ALL RELIGIONS THE SAME?

1. Hitchens, *God Is Not Great,* 56, 36.
2. Richard Dawkins, *The God Delusion* (New York: Houghton Mifflin, 2006), 36.
3. Daniel C. Dennett, *Breaking the Spell: Religion as a Natural Phenomenon* (New York, Penguin Books: 2006), 9.
4. Mahatma Gandhi, quoted in M. S. Mehendale's *Gandhi Looks at Leprosy* as cited at http://www.reference.com/browse/wiki/Father_Damien.
5. Hitchens, *God Is Not Great,* 25.

NOTES

CHAPTER 2: ISN'T RELIGION JUST
WISHFUL THINKING?

1. Hitchens, *God Is Not Great,* 4.
2. Voltaire, *Épître à l'Auteur du Livre des Trois Imposteurs* ("Letter to the author of *The Three Impostors*"), November 10, 1770. This statement by Voltaire became so familiar that Gustave Flaubert included it in his *Dictionnaire des idées reçues* ("Dictionary of commonplace ideas"), and it is still among the most frequently quoted of Voltaire's dicta.
3. Sigmund Freud, *Totem and Taboo* (New York: W. W. Norton, 1962).
4. Paul C. Vitz, *Faith of the Fatherless: The Psychology of Atheism* (Dallas: Spence Publishing, 1999), see especially 6–16.

CHAPTER 4: CAN A PERSON BE MORALLY
GOOD WITHOUT RELIGION?

1. Though this well-known maxim is not an exact quotation of Dostoyevsky, it accurately encapsulates the belief espoused by Ivan Karamazov in the early chapters of *The Brothers Karamazov*. Ivan has concluded that there is no God and no immortality. He then claims that as a logical consequence, "everything is lawful." Ivan does say, moreover, "If there is no immortality, there is no virtue."
2. George Washington, Farewell address to his cabinet, Philadelphia, Pennsylvania; September 17, 1796.
3. Thomas Jefferson, inscribed on panel three of the Jefferson Memorial in Washington, D.C.

4. James Madison, letter to Frederick Beasley, November 20, 1825, as quoted in *The Founders' Almanac,* 155–156.
5. Hitchens, *God Is Not Great,* 27.

CHAPTER 6: ARE RELIGIOUS PEOPLE LESS INTELLIGENT THAN NONBELIEVERS?

1. Sam Harris, *Letter to a Christian Nation* (New York: Knopf, 2006), xi.
2. Dawkins, *The God Delusion,* 1200.
3. Richard Dawkins, "Bible Belter," *The Times Literary Supplement*, September 5, 2007.
4. Mother Teresa, address given at Harvard's Class Day Exercises, June 9, 1982; http://www.columbia.edu/cu/augustine/arch/teresa82.html.

PART II: RELIGION AND SOCIETY

1. Hitchens, *God Is Not Great,* 56.

CHAPTER 7: DOES RELIGION DO MORE HARM THAN GOOD?

1. Hitchens, *God Is Not Great,* 176.

CHAPTER 8: DOESN'T RELIGION CAUSE WAR AND VIOLENCE?

1. Ross Douthat, "Lord Have Mercy," *The Claremont Review of Books,* Summer 2007.
2. See http://www.salemwitchtrials.com/faqs.html#victims.
3. See, for instance, http://wiki.answers.com/Q/How_many_people_died_from_the_Inquisition.

4. For a more precise breakdown of the deaths from atheist regimes, see http://www.hawaii.edu/powerkills/NOTE1.HTM, which puts the figure at over 130 million.

5. See the statistics given by R. J. Rummel in his book *Death by Government* (New Brunswick, NJ: Transaction Publishers, 1994) collected on the Web site http://www.hawaii.edu/powerkills/NOTE1.HTM.

CHAPTER 10: ARE BELIEVERS TRYING TO HASTEN THE END OF THE WORLD?

1. Hitchens, *God Is Not Great,* 56.

CHAPTER 11: IS RELIGIOUS EDUCATION A FORM OF CHILD ABUSE?

1. Hitchens, *God Is Not Great,* 217.
2. Dawkins, *The God Delusion,* 315.
3. Ibid., 317.
4. Hitchens, *God Is Not Great,* 222.

CHAPTER 12: SHOULD BELIEVERS BE ALLOWED TO PROSELYTIZE?

1. Hitchens, *God Is Not Great,* 13, 17, 31.
2. Ann Coulter interviewed by Donny Deutsch on his program *The Big Idea* on CNBC, October 8, 2007; http://www.foxnews.com/story/0,2933,301216,00.html.
3. Cited by Dennis Prager in "Ann Coulter Wants Jews to Become Christian—So What?"; http://www.townhall.com/columnists/DennisPrager/2007/10/16/ann_

coulter_wants_jews_to_become_christian_—_
so_what.
4. Ibid.

CHAPTER 13: HASN'T SCIENCE DISPROVED
GOD'S EXISTENCE?

1. Dawkins, *The God Delusion,* 58–59.
2. Ibid., 71.
3. Ibid., 114.

CHAPTER 14: DOESN'T THE BIBLE MISREPRESENT
THE ORIGINS OF MAN AND THE COSMOS?

1. Hitchens, *God Is Not Great,* 4.
2. Harris, *Letter,* x–xi.
3. Francis S. Collins, *The Language of God: A Scientist Presents Evidence for Belief* (New York: Free Press, 2006), 67.
4. Robert Jastrow, *God and the Astronomers* (New York: W. W. Norton, 1992), 14.
5. Arno Penzias quoted in M. Browne, "Clues to the Universe's Origins Expected," *New York Times,* March 12, 1978. Cited by Francis Collins in *The Language of God,* 76.
6. Dawkins, *The God Delusion,* 113.
7. Collins, *Language of God,* 90.
8. Dawkins, *The God Delusion,* 141.
9. Stephen Hawking, *A Brief History of Time* (New York: Bantam Press, 1998), 144.

NOTES

CHAPTER 15: IS CHRISTIANITY AGAINST SCIENCE?

1. Hitchens, *God Is Not Great,* 229.
2. Dawkins, *The God Delusion,* 126.
3. Hitchens, *God Is Not Great,* 47, 90.
4. See especially Rodney Stark, *For the Glory of God: How Monotheism Led to Reformations, Science, Witch-Hunts, and the End of Slavery* (Princeton, NJ: Princeton University Press, 2003) and *The Victory of Reason: How Christianity Led to Freedom, Capitalism, and Western Success* (New York: Random House, 2005).
5. J. L. Heilbron, Annual Invitation Lecture to the Scientific Instrument Society, Royal Institution, London, December 6, 1995.
6. Hitchens, *God Is Not Great,* 70.
7. Ibid., 64–65.

CHAPTER 16: AREN'T ALL SCIENTISTS AND THINKING PEOPLE ATHEISTS, OR AT LEAST AGNOSTICS?

1. Hitchens, *God Is Not Great,* 229.
2. Address given at a 2005 bioethics conference in Rome at the Regina Apostolorum University, cited in "Feasting on Relics; What Makes a Bioethicist" by Elizabeth Lev, *ZENIT News Service* (March 17, 2005); http://www.zenit.org/article-12538?l=english.
3. John Galbraith Simmons, *The Scientific 100: A Ranking of the Most Influential Scientists, Past and Present* (New York: Citadel Press, 2000).
4. Cited in James E. Force and Richard H. Popkin (eds.), *Newton and Religion: Context, Nature and Influ-*

ence, International Archives of the History of Ideas (Springer Science+Business Media, 1999), 233.

5. Quoted in Des MacHale, *Wisdom* (Cork: Mercier Press, 2002).

6. J. H. Tiner, *Louis Pasteur–Founder of Modern Medicine* (Milford, MI: Mott Media, 1990), 90.

7. Hitchens, *God Is Not Great,* 92.

8. Stephen Jay Gould, "Impeaching a Self-Appointed Judge," *Scientific American,* July 1992, 267(1):118–121.

9. Edward J. Larson, Larry Witham, "Scientists Are Still Keeping the Faith," *Nature* 386 (6624), April 3, 1997, 435–436.

10. James H. Leuba, *The Belief in God and Immortality: A Psychological, Anthropological and Statistical Study* (Boston: Sherman, French & Co., 1916).

CHAPTER 17: IS RELIGIOUS FAITH IRRATIONAL?

1. Hitchens, *God Is Not Great,* 255, 5.

2. Ibid., 185.

3. See especially Thomas Aquinas, *Summa Theologiae* Ia, q. 2, a. 3.

4. Dawkins, *The God Delusion,* 77.

5. Pope John Paul II, encyclical letter *Fides et Ratio,* September 14, 1998, no. 43.

6. Hitchens, *God Is Not Great,* 5.

7. Dawkins, *The God Delusion,* 51.

8. Ibid., 56.

NOTES

PART IV: CHRISTIANITY UNDER FIRE

1. Dawkins, *The God Delusion,* 31.

CHAPTER 18: IS THE GOD OF THE BIBLE
A JEALOUS SADIST?

1. Dawkins, *The God Delusion,* 31.
2. Ibid., 19, 38, 46.

CHAPTER 19: ARE THE GOSPELS RELIABLE
HISTORICAL DOCUMENTS?

1. Hitchens, *God Is Not Great,* 111, 120.
2. Dawkins, *The God Delusion,* 92–93.
3. Second Vatican Council, Dogmatic Constitution on Divine Revelation *Dei Verbum* (November 18, 1965), no. 19.
4. Dawkins, *The God Delusion,* 95.
5. Ibid., 96–97.
6. Craig L. Blomberg, *The Historical Reliability of the Gospels* (Downers Grove, IL: InterVarsity Press, 1987); F. F. Bruce, *The New Testament Documents: Are They Reliable?* 5th ed. (Downers Grove, IL: InterVarsity Press, 1983).

CHAPTER 20: DID THE HISTORICAL
JESUS REALLY EXIST?

1. Dawkins, *The God Delusion,* 97.
2. Hitchens, *God Is Not Great,* 114, 117.
3. Theodore Dalrymple, "Oh, to Be in England: What the New Atheists Don't See," *The City Journal* 17/4 (Autumn 2007); http://www.city-journal.org/html/17_4_oh_to_be.html.

4. Tacitus, *Annals* 15.39–43.

5. Suetonius, *Lives of the Caesars,* "Claudius" 5.25.4.

6. Julius Africanus, *Extant Writings,* XVIII in The Ante-Nicene Fathers, ed. by Alexander Roberts and James Donaldson (Grand Rapids: Eerdmans, 1973), vol. VI, 130, as cited in Gary R. Habermas, *The Historical Jesus: Ancient Evidence for the Life of Christ* (Joplin, MO: College Press Publishing Company, 1996).

7. Pliny, *Letters,* transl. by William Melmoth, rev. by W. M. L. Hutchinson (Cambridge: Harvard University Press, 1935), vol. II, X:96, cited in Habermas, *The Historical Jesus,* 199.

8. Lucian, *The Death of Peregrine,* 11–13, in *The Works of Lucian of Samosata,* transl. by H. W. Fowler and F. G. Fowler, 4 vols. (Oxford: Clarendon, 1949), vol. 4., cited in Habermas, *The Historical Jesus,* 206.

9. Flavius Josephus, *Antiquities* (18:3), quoted in James H. Charlesworth, *Jesus Within Judaism* (Garden City: Doubleday, 1988), 95, cited in Habermas, *The Historical Jesus,* 194.

10. *The Babylonian Talmud,* transl. by I. Epstein (London: Soncino, 1935), vol. III, Sanhedrin 43a, 281, cited in Habermas, *The Historical Jesus,* 203.

CHAPTER 21: DID JESUS FOUND THE CHURCH, OR WAS HE CO-OPTED BY HIS FOLLOWERS?

1. Hitchens, *God Is Not Great,* 114, 120.

CHAPTER 22: DO CHRISTIANS HATE SEX? DOES FAITH ENCOURAGE SEXUAL REPRESSION?

1. Hitchens, *God Is Not Great,* 55, 215, 4.
2. Ibid., 54.
3. See Pope John Paul II, *Man and Woman He Created Them: A Theology of the Body,* transl. by Michael Waldstein (Boston: Pauline Books & Media, 2006).
4. Wendy Shalit, *A Return to Modesty: Discovering the Lost Virtue* (New York: Free Press, 1999).
5. Robert T. Michael, John H. Gagnon, and Gina Kolata, *Sex in America* (Boston: Little, Brown and Company, 1994).
6. Bernard Spilka, *The Psychology of Religion: An Empirical Approach* (New York: Guilford Press, 2003), 186.
7. Hitchens, *God Is Not Great,* 40.

CHAPTER 23: ARE ATHEISTS MORE TOLERANT THAN BELIEVERS?

1. Hitchens, *God Is Not Great,* 13.
2. Harris, *Letter,* vii.
3. Hitchens, *God Is Not Great,* 56, 64, 32, 192, 184, 54.
4. Sam Harris, *The End of Faith: Religion, Terror, and the Future of Reason* (New York: W. W. Norton, 2005), 14, 15, 46.
5. Ibid., 52–53.
6. Theodore Dalrymple, "What the New Atheists Don't See: To Regret Religion Is to Regret Western Civilization," *City Journal,* August 2007.
7. Harris, *The End of Faith,* 45.
8. Hitchens, *God Is Not Great,* 9, emphasis added.

CHAPTER 24: ARE ATHEISTS BETTER CITIZENS
THAN RELIGIOUS FOLK?

1. John Locke, *A Letter Concerning Toleration,* ed. and introduced by James Tully (Indianapolis: Hackett Publishing Company, 1983), 51.

2. Cited by Peter Hitchens, "Hitchens vs Hitchens," *The Daily Mail* (December 21, 2007), http://www.dailymail.co.uk/pages/live/articles/news/newscomment.html?in_article_id=459427&in_page_id=1787&in_a_source.

CHAPTER 25: ARE ATHEISTS MORE ETHICAL
THAN RELIGIOUS BELIEVERS?

1. Hitchens, *God Is Not Great,* 74, 91.

2. Peter Hitchens, "Hitchens vs Hitchens."

3. Richard Dawkins, "Let's All Stop Beating Basil's Car," *Edge: The World Question Center,* 2006: http://www.edge.org/q2006/q06_9.html.

4. Hitchens, *God Is Not Great,* 214, 87.

5. Dawkins, *The God Delusion,* 215.

CHAPTER 26: ARE ATHEISTS HAPPIER
THAN BELIEVERS?

1. Hitchens, *God Is Not Great,* 16.

2. My thanks to Arthur C. Brooks for his enlightening *Wall Street Journal* article "The Ennui of Saint Teresa (September 24, 2007, A18), where he gathers some of the statistics I have cited here.

3. Ibid.

4. See http://www.cfsv.org/communitysurvey/.

5. Ibid.

6. Ibid.

CHAPTER 27: ARE ATHEISTS MORE GENEROUS AND PHILANTHROPIC THAN THEIR RELIGIOUS COUNTERPARTS?

1. Hitchens, *God Is Not Great,* 5.

2. http://www.cfsv.org/communitysurvey/.

3. Arthur C. Brooks, "Religious Faith and Charitable Giving," *Policy Review* 121, October/November 2003.

4. Ibid.

5. Ibid.

6. Ibid.

7. Voltaire cited in Michael Davies, *For Altar and Throne: The Rising in the Vendée* (St. Paul, MN: Remnant Press, 1997), 13.

8. Brooks, "Religious Faith."